Counterfeit Culture

by Keith Brown

Contents

Dedication

Especially to Jonathan, my son of courage.

You never stopped being a faithful son, no matter how many times we slammed the door in your face. Thank you for helping us learn how to forgive.

To all my children.

For graciously putting up with parents who thought we knew what was best for you, but to our fault and your hurt, we put the opinions of others above our love for you. We love your unique selves more than we can express!

To my sister Leigh

and to all the unnamed warriors.

Thank you for relentlessly praying, even when it seemed nothing was happening.

God is restoring the years the locusts have eaten!

Preface

In 1989, my husband and I joined a religious cult. Most of the thirty years we were there, we thought we were right. We escaped in 2018 after some painful events that opened our eyes to the fact that we had traded the truth for a lie. We had lost the joy we had known before, and replaced it with rules and regulations that changed with one person's whims. The hardest truth to face was that we'd been duped and had wasted thirty years of our lives! Between the first moment of our eyes being opened to the day we left, we agonized about walking away from it. We had two brief departures, kind of practice runs for the final fleeing.

Some of you may wonder, "Well, why didn't you just walk away the moment you wanted to?"

Just as it's hard to leave other abusive situations, it's hard to leave a cult. Our hearts, minds, and emotions were totally invested. And we had given most of our assets to the cult. During this uncertain time of wanting to leave, I'd often hear my mother say, "We often choose a familiar pain over an unfamiliar joy."

How true. I wanted to leave but felt fearful of the unknown. Who would be our friends? Where would we go? What would happen to our kids? So many unanswered questions, all based in fear. I actually admitted that I feared no one would come to my funeral! But we'd been living in fear for thirty years. It was just that the familiar fear at Homestead seemed safer than the unknown fears if we left. I thought a cult had to be all bad, so I wrestled between being grateful for the good things and feeling guilty for desperately wanting out.

This tug of war took its toll on every aspect of our family. The constant fear of going to hell if I "broke my covenant" kept me company as my fate hung in the balance. My mind would say, "But there is good here," and then feel confused until something would happen that seemed explicitly wrong, and I'd want to beat the exit door down and run out.

This wrestling between the good and evil lasted long after we left. It has taken a long time to be rid of the guilt and condemnation that have been my companions for so long. I remember the founder saying on numerous occasions that the best counterfeits are those that seem so close to the truth. Homestead looked so good on the outside, so safe and wholesome. But like trying to pay for a plane ticket with forged money, your dream vacation was just that: a dream. A longing for something you hoped for but never experienced. My experience in Homestead was the truth of the Proverb that says, "Hope deferred makes the heart sick."

Hope kept being deferred for a long time until I could no longer justify staying. It was then that I realized my hope had been in the wrong thing. I wanted to be loved, and I wanted a safe place to raise my children. And as I said, there were good things at Homestead. I learned valuable lessons and my children learned how to work hard. I am grateful for those things, even though what I experienced at the end of living in this counterfeit culture was *rejection, fear, and despair*. I watched my children slip and fall as they tried to navigate how to live life outside the restrictions and limits their lives had been defined by. Outside of Homestead, I quickly realized why so many who leave situations like ours reject everything that reminds them of the life they lived. Even the good things.

This book started out as a letter to my children. It was my effort to bring clarity to why we rejected what we had drilled into them their whole lives. I felt compelled to write my jumbled thoughts and feelings so that maybe I could make sense of it all.

During the thirty years of captivity, I could so easily quote John 8:32, *The truth will set you free,* but I found myself bound in invisible shackles. Alone. When the bubble burst and I had to admit I'd been duped, shame and regret haunted me. My lifelong enemy, condemnation, tried to punish me. Nothing seemed worse than having to admit I'd wasted thirty years of my life and possibly ruined all nine of my children's lives.

As I began untangling the web of lies that I had desperately clung to, the truth began to not only reveal itself but *actually set me free.* I could see how my insecurity and desire to be loved led to me joining a cult. I saw how during my time there I gradually surrendered my identity, mind, beliefs, and family to leaders who convinced me that my loyalty *to them* was the only way to honor God. I fell under their control and abuse and lived under their false pretense of security.

When we are insecure, we have a tendency to rob someone else's identity to make us feel better. Or sometimes we feel ashamed and condemned and think we *deserve* ill treatment. Sometimes we decide to control others, using our God-given gifts to tear others down rather than building them up. In doing this, we can fall into abusive patterns. Abuse, whether it's physical, sexual, verbal, or spiritual, shuts down our ability to be the people God created us to be. This is true in jobs, marriages, families, *and* churches.

All my life I had been frantically trying to keep up appearances, to look confident and secure. It was a lot of work, and I never felt like I was successful. In my search for truth these past years, I discovered what God means when He says, *Come to me, all you who are weary and burdened, and I will give you rest. Matthew 11:28-30 (NIV)* It took a crisis for those words to become flesh within me.

Through telling my story, I hope to offer hope, redemption, restoration, and peace to counteract despair, deprivation, destruction, and confusion. We only have one life to live, so whether we are young, old, or in the middle, now is the time to take back lost ground and find out who we are. I hope others can find hope and peace from what I've learned. It's never too late to be set free. It's never too late to start being brutally honest with God. Believe me when I say, *with more light comes more freedom.* Many of you may never have been in a cult or controlling situation before, but any lie we believe can take us down a road of despair. My desire is that this book will bring you encouragement and hope.

My aim is not to shame or blame anyone. This is my story as I lived it. The situations and circumstances are my memories. In facing the truth, I have owned my mistakes. I allowed others to take advantage of my trust, and I ignored lots of red flags. I've forgiven those who hurt me and my children. I see them being just as needy as me. I've asked those I hurt to forgive me for being "one of them." My job is to bless those people I trusted who wronged me and many others, and release them to God.

Jonathan, My Hero

This book is dedicated to our second child, Jonathan, who was seven when we joined Homestead. We expected Jonathan to become a member when he grew up, so we didn't prepare him for anything else. We were not remotely open to the possibility that he could have gifts and talents suited for some vocation other than the few options open to kids at Homestead.

Because his dad and I were sycophants and allowed the leaders to meddle in our family, we allowed them to dictate his life. We put their desires above his. Instead of seeing and meeting his needs, we hurt him repeatedly by rejecting who he was created to be. We thought he was wrong to leave us and enter what we called "the world," a place Homestead intentionally kept kids unprepared for.

What we didn't know was that Jonathan wanted to be a Marine. He is an exceptional warrior, a freedom fighter, and my hero. He has persevered and overcome many obstacles in his life. God's angels have kept him safe through severely dangerous situations in Iraq, Afghanistan, and the Philippines, where he bravely defended our country. More than that, he courageously defended us when we least deserved it. Even when we weren't there for him, he was always waiting for us to see the light. It turns out he was right all along. He never rejected us, and he always obeyed the command to honor his father and mother. At eighteen, he found the courage to jump into the unknown and pave the way for us to take the leap 16 years later.

To my other wonderful, resilient children, I am utterly amazed that you still love us. You have proven over and over again that God makes all things new. We've had to tackle hard things together but look what God has done because when we didn't deserve it, you forgave us for raising you like you were in boot camp instead of the loving home you deserved. Nothing makes me happier than getting to be with you. No expectations, just being together. I have loved watching your unique gifts and callings blossom in your lives. Even more, I love watching each of you laugh as you interact with one another. I feel like God has mercifully knit us back together. Now I get the privilege of watching you love your kids like I wish I had loved you.

If ever I complain to God for not answering my prayers quickly enough, I thank Him for all the friends, family, and people I don't know, who prayed for us to have the courage to do what Jonathan did at eighteen. The prayers built a giant memorial that grew so tall it toppled over the fortress of blinding self-righteousness I had erected around myself. Only then was I able to see the truth and to be set free.

This is a condensed story of what I experienced, how I fell into captivity, and how God opened my eyes to see His truth. No matter the situation or circumstance we find ourselves in, the solution isn't about demanding our rights! It's about realizing that if the Spirit of God resides inside us, we are to let Him in on what we have been dishonest about. Let's give Him room and time, and let's come clean and face the truth. I know from experience, *The truth will set you free. John 8:32 (NIV)*

Part One

Counterfeit Culture

10/28/2018

Tomorrow I will attend my last meeting. The thought makes my stomach churn. Realizing I might hyperventilate, I tell myself to take a deep breath and will one foot in front of the other only to wander around the house in circles. I can't stand the thought of packing up the house filled with 29 years of memories and stuff accumulated in the years of raising nine children. I want to curl up into a catatonic ball. After tomorrow, no one in the community will be allowed to help me pack, including my own daughter. That would be too awkward anyway. We'll be dubbed "Judases, enemies of God" and when I see any of them in town, they'll turn their faces away and shun me. I won't be able to blame them. I did that to others who left. Our leaving means we've "broken our covenant" with Homestead. And it's the ultimate sin in this community.

Some will be shocked to see the Browns have fallen and are on their way to Hell. The leaders won't, though. They know we've been hanging on by a thread. They know we don't trust them anymore. The veil has been lifted from our eyes and while that breach was sometimes patched up, it was never fully repaired. Their job now will be to convince the congregation how far we've fallen and to put fear into anyone thinking of joining us. They'll band tightly together knowing they are always right, and we were wrong.

Remorse floods me as I realize the truth for the millionth time that I've wasted thirty years of my life at Homestead. We gave them everything we had, including the land they call Brazos de Dios ("The Arms of God").

This house is no longer home. It feels nothing remotely like the arms of God now that I understand God doesn't shame us and humiliate us and smother us.

I've spent years afraid to stay and afraid to go; the fear of the unknown grips my chest once more. I take a deep breath. Tomorrow will be the last time I have to endure a Sunday meeting.

Growing Up and Mam'selle

"Rat-a-tat-tat, rat-a-tat-tat" hammered the drums followed by the theme song from the Music Man. "Seventy-six trombones" blared through the intercom speakers in my bedroom. Or it could have been the theme song from, "Stop the World, I want to get off," or "Hello Dolly." That was how I woke up every day as a child. I don't remember ever having an alarm clock. Showtunes from whatever Broadway play my mother had recently seen on her quarterly buying trips to New York became the alarm that woke my sister Leigh and me.

I grew up in Chickasaw Gardens in Memphis, Tennessee. A wonderland of a neighborhood. Our thoroughly modern mother designed our Memphis home in the 1950's with floor-to-ceiling plate glass windows. She covered the floors with the latest shag carpet and installed built-in couches. A twenty-foot balcony connected two bedrooms upstairs and hung above the middle of the house. We could look down and see the dining room in one direction and the entrance hall in the other. For some reason our mother allowed us to put a trampoline on the balcony. Or maybe she didn't notice. Huge elephant ears and tropical plants rose up from a little garden plot she planted under her signature floating staircase, and every time I sat in my seat at the dining room table, I had to move a big leaf out of my way.

It was a safe neighborhood, and we knew all the kids who lived there. We ran in and out of each other's houses, had high-jumping competitions using bushes for crossbars, made mud forts at the lake around the corner, and blasted each other with mud balls. Mama could tell mesmerizing stories, which, I think, is why I loved acting out plays so much. We put on "The Sound of Music" in Cathy Reed's garage. Cathy and my sister Leigh fought over who would portray Maria. I was Gretl, because I was the youngest. Our production ended abruptly when the garage door broke and fell down.

My mother perpetually ran late, as though she could defy time. She wanted to live on her timetable and by her rules, which didn't coincide with the school bell or speed limits. I don't know how many planes waited for my mother to arrive at the gate, but I do remember one that came back to the gate to get her.

My class at school was divided into sections A and B. We called section A the "smart section" and Section B the "dumb section." I was the dumbest person in the smart section. For all her eccentricity, my mother was intelligent and realized early on that I was dyslexic. I clearly remember taking spelling tests and spelling every word correctly but backwards. I couldn't understand why I kept flunking. My mother hired a tutor and even though I eventually became a great speller, I also became afraid to try anything new. Instead, I stuck to things I was good at, like sports and dancing. Ever since I was young, I've been terrified of failing and longed for others' approval. Fear of failing and trying to keep my mother happy became the scaffolding around my life that would eventually make me prey to a cult where I didn't have to think or try anything new. My mother wasn't afraid to try and fail. She always used to say, "It's okay to fail. That's how we learn."

But I never truly believed it. Not for myself.

Perhaps that was due to growing up with a mother who was nothing like the other women of her time. My friends' moms greeted their kids with an after-school snack and a hug. I came home to an empty house because my mother was a workaholic, which was unusual for the 1960s. That may be part of the reason I played so many sports after school. Flossie, my absolute favorite person in the world and our housekeeper, frequently left us turnip or collard greens from her garden on the stove. Mama rarely cooked. When she did, she had an interesting repertoire consisting of tuna fish, creamed peas, French toast, escargot, and she made a pot roast every other year. I don't remember her ever eating a meal. Even at Thanksgiving she served the food, but never sat down to eat.

Mama had a sweet tooth beyond anyone I've ever known. As a child, she was allowed to have dessert once a week, so she vowed when she became an adult, she would eat dessert whenever she wanted. And she stuck to her vow. On rare occasions, she would line every flat surface in the house with wax paper and, after stirring for hours, I'd watch her plop spoonful after spoonful of fluffy white blobs of divinity, filled with what she said were the perfect black walnuts, onto the wax paper. I don't remember her giving much of it away, but I do remember her eating it. Years later when my mother asked my husband Curtis, who is an estate planning attorney, what he'd like to inherit from her, his response was, "Your pancreas."

My grandmother frequently brought us a chicken dinner with baked cauliflower, cabbage, and her famous rolls. I don't know whether Mama asked her to bring dinner regularly or if Grandmama worried about us developing diabetes.

My mother, Bettye Jo was a driven woman, and her father was her first driver. By her sixth birthday, Mama's father, a dentist, began grooming her to be a competitive tennis player. He pushed her hard to win, despite having no natural athletic ability or rhythm. She learned to play by sheer determination to avoid her father's sharp disapproval. Like a whip cracking over her head, she commanded her rather spastic self to put topspin on a forehand and hit a deadly backhand, securing both city and state championships. To prove it, we had shelves lined with an assortment of brass ladies holding tennis rackets in various poses.

Mama had two birth certificates, one year apart, though I never understood why. One explanation she gave was that her restless and demanding father, who saw his daughter as a bright, intelligent, and curious child, decided she was ready for school earlier than the other kids her age. I wondered if he bribed someone at the Bureau of Statistics to make her a new birth certificate.

For college, Mama went to Baylor University in Waco, Texas, on a tennis scholarship, but I don't think Baylor reformed her in the way Grandmama was hoping. Though she was attending a Christian college, my mother hated the Baptist church because of their pro-segregation stance. When she was still in Memphis, she took a group of black kids to church one Sunday. When they were asked to leave, she took them fishing instead and made up her mind then and there that she'd never go to church again.

In her sophomore year of college, Mama's father had his leg amputated, developed gangrene, and died of complications. At the age of 19, Mama left Baylor and moved back to Memphis. Her father had made clear to Mama that since she was the oldest, she would take over his dental practice in case anything ever happened to him. She suddenly became responsible for her two siblings and her mother. She hired a dentist and dental students from the University of Tennessee to run the practice, while she attended a seminar at the famous Peabody Hotel and learned how to make a new type of denture. She worked herself to exhaustion working late nights making dentures. As I said, she had no fear of trying something new.

She had the tenacity of a mountain lion, and her fear of being poor propelled her down a path to make money. By the time her dental office was shut down, she had made enough money to buy a small apartment complex for her mother. When I was young, I'd go with Grandmama on Saturday mornings to collect the rent. The rent money was what she lived on. Mama also earned herself a complete mental and physical breakdown. Instead of pursuing her lifelong dream of owning a high fashion boutique, she married someone with money who would take care of her. Her first husband, a doctor, had the means for her to rest and recover from her breakdown, but after seven years, she felt restless and smothered. She filed for divorce and reclaimed ownership of her life.

As the story goes, my tall, dark, and handsome daddy snagged my mother on the tennis court in Memphis. After marrying him, Mama's dream of opening a fashion boutique came true. In 1951, she opened Mam'selle on Union Avenue in a rambling, multi-split-level building with the motto, "Fashion for the Young Sophisticate" inscribed on the sign.

This old building had floors under the shag carpet that creaked like a storm-tossed ship. She covered the walls in burlap where she displayed complete outfits, accessories and all. To keep the carpet clean, Mama asked her customers to take off their shoes, leave them at the door, and don a pair of Chinese-looking slippers she provided in a big basket near the door.

The majority of the clothes were on the upper level of the store, but the dressing rooms were on the first level. To try on clothes, women were encouraged to do so on the second floor, out in the open. Men were not allowed on the upper levels, though there were a few times a red-faced man escaped notice and was promptly chased back down the steps.

On Saturdays at Mam'selle, Mama made and served tuna fish sandwiches to the employees. After lunch, she would light a long incense stick and traipse around the store to get rid of the smell. I don't know which smelled worse, the tuna or the mixture of incense and tuna.

One of the women Mama hired to manage Mam'selle was a beautiful young Black woman named Alma. When she went on buying trips to New York, Alma would accompany her, and they would share a hotel room. It was the 1960s in Tennessee and people frowned on Mama for being in such close proximity with a Black woman. But Mama adored

Alma and ignored the derogatory comments. She was always ahead of her time. Being a good judge of character, she had some loyal employees who I claimed as family. To Mama's credit she would fight for any one of them if there was a hint of injustice.

My mother loved a bargain, and she found one when she planned a family vacation to the Caribbean. During the Cuban Missile Crisis! I think there was a write up in the Commercial Appeal fashion section about what we were wearing the day we left. Mama said everyone treated us suspiciously, like we were spies. On the way home the pilot wandered into Cuban airspace and the Cubans forced the plane to either land or be shot down, as I recall the story. I was only four but heard the story many times. They emptied the entire plane and searched through everything. My dad had bought a wooden crate of rum, and they made him open it with his bare hands. I don't know if he got to keep the rum or not. My terrified parents stood paralyzed while soldiers threatened them with bayonets. We listened to gunfire all day. Who cared how fashionable our clothes were if we were going to be stabbed to death on the tarmac in Havana! That vacation 'valya' (as my kids imitate my mom's southern pronunciation of "value") almost cost us our lives, but it made a great story!

Mama was heartbroken when Alma suddenly moved to Michigan when her husband got a job there. Over the years they lost contact. Fifty years later when Mama was in her eighties, a longtime friend from Chickasaw Gardens was taking care of her in the hospital. The phone rang and our friend answered the call. When she hung up Mama asked her who had called and she said, "It was Honeybunch." (that was Leigh's nickname)

The attending nurse looked up startled and said, "Are you Mrs. Schopfer?" Mama said, "Yes."

The nurse said, "Mrs. Schopfer, I'm Alma's daughter! She was just wondering if you were still alive. She's coming to see me in July. I know she'd love to see you!"

This was April and Alma felt like July would be too late, so she came to Memphis to see Mama a month later. They hugged and cried and reminisced after all those years. Two months later, due to advanced Parkinson's, Mama could no longer talk, and we moved her to Waco. Alma was right. July would have been too late.

Jesus

My mother refused to be part of the Baptist church, so the only religious reference I had as a child was the Catholic church my dad took me to. I liked Mass because even though it was in Latin and I couldn't understand a word they were saying, it was short. Afterward we would go to IHOP for pancakes. I took confirmation classes and nervously confessed my sins to a priest behind the screen in a dark booth. I always confessed lying as my last sin because most of my confessions were made up.

Daddy grew up in New Orleans in a Catholic family, was taught by nuns in a Catholic school, and earned a scholarship to Tulane for his tennis and basketball skills. All he knew of religion was the Catholic church. His parents were disappointed that he had chosen a non-Catholic for a wife, but they weren't nearly as disappointed as my Baptist grandmother was that her daughter had chosen a Catholic. That was complete heresy to her.

Daddy felt we needed to go to church and knew Mama would never take us, so he took me to be baptized when I was six. It was just Daddy, a priest wearing a cream-colored robe, and me. Daddy held me over what looked like a white marble bird bath while the priest poured water over my forehead. He handed me a large wooden cross with a man nailed to it, which I hung over my bed when I got home. I didn't know anything about religion or church or God for that matter, but after the priest baptized me, I felt in my six-year-old heart like there was something big and mysterious all around me and it had something to do with that cross and the sad man hanging on it.

I feared dropping my Bible because the Catholic church told me it was a mortal sin and would send me straight to Hell. My grandmother, who could be sweet and loving, had another side to her. She seethed underneath her saintly appearance when I was baptized as a Catholic. She whined about my mother not going to church and condemned her to Hell for her rebellion so many times my mother forbade her to be around us for a long time. For a while I became scared of dying, which possibly came from those arguments about religion between my mother and grandmother. None of the talk about church in my life had anything to do with the man on the cross. Maybe that's why he was sad.

My sister Leigh was four years older than me. When I was 11, Leigh drove the carpool, so when she started going to Bible study after school, I had to go as well. As I sat in the back of the room, I heard the teacher talking about Jesus, a name I had never heard before. There was something about that name that ripped my heart open. I couldn't stop crying. When I got home, I looked at the cross above my bed and realized that the sad man was Jesus.

As a young teenager I quit the Catholic Church and exchanged it for a Presbyterian one not far from my house where some of my friends went. We roller-skated in the basement and went to retreats where we ate snacks on the bus, sat around a campfire and sang songs like "Pass It On." I didn't think the Presbyterians cared if I dropped my Bible.

From a young age, I was conditioned to believe that my role was to keep my mother happy. I don't know if I was born a people pleaser, or if I learned the trait of trying to keep her and my dad happy, but I grew into a little entertainer. I adored my mother, but at the same time, felt confused by her behavior. The most disconcerting thing about her was how unpredictable she could be. I never knew if she'd be dying in the hospital from some mysterious malady or if she would show up with a brand new, bright red Mercedes. She might announce that she was leaving for Hong Kong one day and then spend three days moaning in bed. As some children tend to do, Leigh and I thought it was somehow our fault, like we were supposed to be mothering her. The lack of stability combined with my fear of failing laid the groundwork for a deep insecurity that would follow me into adulthood.

Though I only remember my parents fighting on a few occasions, a silent iron curtain hung between them. They lived in their separate dismal castles trapped by their own demons and didn't have a clue as to how to get free. My handsome, charming, and funny father, Lou, tried to keep our world in order. Daddy and I were always close. He seemed so normal compared to Mama, and I was sorry that he had to put up with her erratic behavior.

As a teenager, I thought Mama worked too much. What I didn't realize was Mama was taking drugs to keep her going and others to help her sleep and forget. All of them took a toll on her mind and body. I suspected the pharmacist a few doors down from Mam'selle sold her the drugs. Years later, that pharmacist went to prison.

Her behavior grew even more erratic as the years passed. Leigh and I begged Mama to retire, but she drove herself harder and grew more paranoid about people cheating her. Instead of slowing down, she defied Daddy's counsel and franchised Mam'selle by going into partnership with the founder of a big hotel chain. She went from managing two stores in Memphis to thirteen stores around the South. Mama's daring and creativity made me want to be like her, but I hated her dark side.

Daddy started drinking more as I got older. Instead of eating lunch every day he played tennis and often traveled to tournaments all over the country. His amazing athletic skill led to him winning eight prestigious tournaments in two years culminating in the national championship. I imagine he found a refuge in tennis. I once heard him say he owed his life to tennis. Mama's escape was at work and taking more pills.

Occasionally on a Saturday morning, Mama would abruptly wake me up, order me to get dressed. We would go to a mental institution where my aunt had been committed during the night. I hated seeing my beautiful aunt in a straitjacket, completely out of her mind. My mother blamed my aunt's problems on her drug addiction, but never faced the fact that she was an addict herself. We always thought because she was the oldest that she felt it was her duty to take care of her siblings, but I wonder if it was the guilt of getting her sister hooked on drugs that drove her.

When Leigh went away to college I became my mother's sidekick diet companion. Though neither of us needed to lose weight, I joined her because that was our mother/daughter time. I took up the mantle and became obsessed. I found her approval by keeping myself thin and trying to be pretty. Mama said she was trying to live up to the motto the American socialite and wife of King Edward VIII, Wallis Simpson, coined, "You can never be too rich or too thin."

One time she gave me diet pills that she called black mollies. I took one and stayed awake for four days. I figured that must be what she was taking to keep her awake most nights when she was on a buying trip in New York. On those trips with her I felt guilty for needing food and sleep! We tried every diet she could find; we had acupuncture knobs put in our ears that we were instructed to turn when we got hungry, and one time we went to Memphis State to be hypnotized into not eating. The hypnotist looked at her and told her she needed a psychiatrist. On one diet we'd eat only hard-boiled eggs and drink sherry. (I was only a teenager) Another time we spent time in ketosis eating only bacon and pork rinds.

Mama lived her entire life trying to escape from not being good enough. Condemnation and fear whipped her in a never-ending circle. She was the classic enabler driven by guilt. I'm certain she was being chased by the demons of approval and the fear of feeling pain. She only felt she measured up when someone told her she was beautiful or successful, and that was only a brief reprieve. Then she was off again, working herself to death. She couldn't bear to be still and listen to the voices in her head. When the demons came calling, she would end up in the hospital with a mysterious illness. Leigh and I always worried she was going to die.

Since Leigh was older than me, I spent my teenage years without her support and living with two miserable people. I had a lot of questions. With all my striving to fit in and make people happy, I felt empty and alone. If that was all there was to life, I wasn't sure I wanted to live. I needed direction and hope. I desperately wanted to know if there was more to God than what I had experienced. I hoped God would give me some answers. One night I had a life-altering experience. I found myself kneeling by my bed asking God to prove He was real. I don't know how long I was on my knees, but when I opened my eyes, my hands were in the air like a child reaching up for her daddy, and I was making sounds I didn't understand. I was alone but completely enveloped by light and love. Tears streamed down my face, and I knew He was real.

The next day I flunked an Algebra test, my boyfriend broke up with me, and my grandmother told me I had encountered the devil. It didn't take long to realize that, in spite of that amazing experience, I still might flunk Algebra if I didn't study, and maybe I should keep that God-experience to myself before everyone thought I was crazy.

My prayer life matured slowly. Two years after that experience I told the Lord I would go to whatever college accepted me the next Saturday. Believe it or not, I received an acceptance letter from LSU that Saturday! I wonder if I would have not gone to college at all if I hadn't gotten that letter. I think God knew that years later I'd desperately need an old college friend, so He answered my crazy prayer. When I asked my daddy what to major in, he responded, "Whatever makes you happy." Maybe he said that because that's what he wanted: to be happy.

A Good Catch

I wore a lime green, shirtwaist dress and clear plastic wedge sandals underneath my graduation gown when I crossed the stage my last day at Louisiana State University. I opened my diploma and found a parking ticket with a note saying I would be issued my diploma after I paid the fine. And with that, my four-year vacation came to an end.

After one last Po-boy sandwich, Mama whisked me away to Dallas to help her finish the work on her new store in NorthPark Mall in Dallas, Texas, so she could open it by the end of the summer. Since I had spent four years doing whatever made me happy at my parents' expense, I felt obligated to work for her. If I did anything else, I'd be letting her down. The old habit of trying to please her kept the fear of failing at bay. That summer Mama and I lived in an apartment complex occupied by young people whose perpetual parties kept us awake every night.

I had grown up doing odd jobs for her at her store in Memphis, but this was my first paying job, and my mother worked me hard. She expected nothing less from her daughter. As a child, my first job ever was picking straight pins out of the carpet at Mam'selle. Those Chinese slippers had soft soles, and Mama didn't want her customers getting stuck with a pin. After that, Mama said she would pay the girls in our neighborhood a nickel for every necklace or bracelet we untangled. I gathered my friends up and we went to work, but I don't think any of us ever got paid. All the experience of getting knots out of the costume jewelry did give me a knack for untangling things, though. Always a good talent when you end up with nine kids.

I also delivered the clothes requiring alterations to Mrs. Rushing who worked in the small attic at the top of the building. I don't remember her saying a word, but that might be because I never stopped talking long enough to let her. At another point in my young career, I learned to make three-part tickets on a machine I called 'Tilly the Ticket Maker' and then fasten them to each new garment. If I didn't have tickets to make, I would try on clothes and be a nuisance while I waited for a ride to the University Club so I could go swimming or play tennis.

But now, with a college education in my pocket, I was ready for bigger jobs. Instead, my first assignment was to cover wood posts with fabric and walls with burlap. When the store opened Leigh found her niche as a manager. I never enjoyed sales, but Leigh consistently sold more than anyone else who worked at Mam'selle. She was always able to convince customers to buy whatever she suggested.

Watching Leigh outperform at Mam'selle, I realized I didn't have a backup plan for my life. There was a time when I wanted to be an occupational therapist or a photographer, but I never had the confidence to pursue either. At one point I considered moving to New Orleans to start nursing school, but decided I wasn't up for starting all over. Looking back, I think I was just aimless. I didn't realize it then, but I would have benefited from someone taking me by the hand and guiding me into a life's purpose.

Mama and I left Leigh in Dallas, and I landed back in Memphis working at Mam'selle. The cold war between my parents had escalated into the frozen zone while I had partied my way through four years at LSU. Mama decided she wanted to contract with a manufacturer in Hong Kong to produce her own line of clothing. It didn't matter how much Daddy drank or yelled, "You are not going to Hong Kong!" Mama stood stone still, unnervingly silent. I knew that look from her. She would be on the next plane to Hong Kong as soon as she could book it. That independent streak marked her success in business and her failure in relationships.

The harder she fought my dad, the more she seemed to withdraw from the relationships that offered her the most support. With her as the prominent figure in my life, my own social life became almost as confusing as my parents' relationship. Upon my return to Memphis, I renewed a relationship that had ended in high school and found myself very quickly engaged to be married, even though something felt off in my heart. I didn't know what to do. I told Daddy, "I don't know why, but I don't think I should marry him," and he responded with rare but needed advice, "Don't marry him. Do what your heart is telling you."

My mother's advice was, "Honey, nothing lasts forever!" In other words, "You can always get a divorce."

***

I watched Mama chase her dreams of building a chain of successful innovative dress shops, doggedly determined nothing would stop her. Leigh and I begged her to slow down and rest, but she relentlessly pushed herself and everyone around her. Mama was driven by a strong force that whipped her forward. As my months at home went on, Mama's erratic behavior and my inability to express what I felt eventually led me to hate her. Through my eyes, she couldn't do anything right. She could have told me, "I love you," and given me a million dollars, and I would have resented it. That's what bitterness does. I was living proof of the saying, "I'll drink the poison and hope it kills you."

On one of our many buying trips to the Dallas Apparel Mart, Mama and I stood outside the doors to the Kim Dawson modeling agency. I held my briefcase under my arm as models rushed out the doors headed for the runway. Mama said something to me that made me so mad I wanted to take my briefcase and hit her with it. Literally. In the middle of all the clamor, I heard God say, "You be thankful for your mother!"

I suddenly felt very small and contrite. I couldn't deny that voice. All of a sudden, God broke into my stony, cold heart - I knew I had a choice to make. I began a campaign to be thankful for my mother. I felt like a baby training for an Ironman triathlon. That's how hard it was.

For the next two years, every time hatred rose up in my heart, I would thank God for her, praising Him no matter what I felt, most times not meaning the words I spoke. It was an act of my will, an act of obedience. Though it was exhausting to consistently choose to be thankful for her, something incredible happened: I developed an honest relationship with God. I'd talk to Him about how I didn't feel any love for my mother and that I needed His help. Soon I began to see her like God saw her, as a broken, hurt, and confused woman who needed help. Over time I began to love her and have compassion for her. She was scared and running away from pain and trauma by working hard and driving those around her. I also saw the truth about myself: I was a self-absorbed brat.

Because God kept chipping away at my stony heart, Mama and I grew closer. I began to appreciate the amazing person she was, even though I continued to struggle with my attitude toward her. I always wished she was a different kind of mother. A mother who nurtured me and gave me security. I learned to stop yearning for the mother I wanted and accept the one I had for who she was. I had to quit blaming her for everything and take responsibility for myself. In the training process, I had formed the habit of thanking God for everything; the good, the bad and the confusing. And I had learned to forgive someone who had hurt me, even though it wasn't intentional on her part.

Both lessons helped me put things into God's hands where they belonged. Real joy and true happiness slowly took up residence in my stony heart. Little did I know how important these lessons were in firming my foundation of who I was and who I was meant to be. When God teaches us, we don't easily forget. We may push His lessons aside, but they always surface in the right time, in the right way.

***

In the midst of learning to love my mother, I decided to take my dad's advice, and to my friends' surprise, I broke off my engagement. Trying to juggle the same old tension at home and ending that relationship called for a fresh start. I left my parents to work out their problems in Memphis and moved into my sister's duplex in Dallas.

I was so excited to work for Leigh. With her I didn't feel like I was riding a never-ending emotional roller coaster, feeling guilty for failing to keep Mama happy. I adored my sister although we are nothing alike. Growing up people would say, "Your sister is so sweet and quiet. Ya'll are so different!" They were right. Leigh made better grades and had a knack for memorizing anything. I thought all her friends were my best friends. When she went off to college and left me alone with my parents, I pined for her. After an eight-year separation I was thrilled to get to live with her. She stayed up half the night and rolled out of bed in time to make the short drive to NorthPark. I went to bed by ten, jumped out of bed early enough to jog a few miles, shower and roll up my hair. We both attended a big Presbyterian church and made lots of friends in the "Bridges" singles' class.

Right off the bat, (no pun intended) in the Fall of 1978, I joined the girls' softball team where I was the left fielder. The coach of our team, Curtis Brown, wore shorts to practice with the oxford cloth shirt he had worn to work. It was obvious he had caught the eye of most girls on the team. He even had a date with my sister Leigh shortly after I moved to Dallas. As usual, I went to bed at ten but couldn't sleep because they were laughing and talking in the living room. Known for giving Leigh's boyfriends a hard time, I yelled from my room, "Go home!"

In spite of that rude introduction, Curtis invited me, along with a lot of others, to a party at his duplex on Binkley Ave. in University Park. I opened his refrigerator and the only thing I found was a 50-pound bag of Arrowhead Mills granola. I instantly assumed he had different dates for lunch and dinner. The party was fun, but when Curtis thought it should end, he removed the bathroom door. That novel idea did the trick. Undaunted that his actions would upset anyone, he smiled and argued confidently with one friend about why the party had to end this way. There was no use arguing with him. He was convinced he was right.

Curtis graduated from Texas Tech where he was the president of his fraternity. He tutored football players because that allowed him to eat better food in the dining room where the football players ate. He skied his way through work at Aspen and Vail as a CPA in the Denver office of Arthur Anderson before going to the University of Texas Law School. Following the same food theme, Curtis showed up at the fraternity house in Austin and asked if he could eat his meals there. The guy who met him at the door said, "Okay," even though their fraternity had no reciprocal dining agreement between campuses, especially for someone who had already completed under-graduate studies.

Curtis made lasting friendships with his new fraternity brothers and started discipling some of them on a regular basis and even had a Bible study at 6 o'clock on Saturday mornings. While Curtis studied on Friday nights, his disciples partied, but the committed ones complied, perhaps as penance, and attended those early Saturday morning studies. One time they went on a camping trip to the Pecos Wilderness mountains. While they climbed a mountain, Curtis decided they should memorize the Sermon on the Mount. His disciples unanimously rebelled. I'm sure he told them that one day they'd regret not committing the most famous sermon in history to memory. After graduating from law school, Curtis moved to Dallas where he made lots of new friends, and reconnected with old ones. He got involved in all sorts of political and nonprofit work in addition to working all hours at a bustling downtown law firm.

Six weeks after I yelled at him to go home, Curtis asked me out on a date to celebrate his brother's birthday with his family. My first impression was that they were so normal, they were almost boring. They seemed happy and genuine, and they all went to the Baptist church. Curtis had grown up going to church with kids whose parents were best friends with his parents. That sounded so stable to me that it took time for me to process that it was genuine. They had absolutely no drama! I couldn't help wondering if they ever got bored.

The next day I left for a sleepless buying trip to New York with Mama. When I got back, Curtis invited me out on our second date. He was a season ticket holder for the Dallas symphony. Perhaps he thought it would impress me, but he soon learned he was wrong. Not long after the musicians took up their instruments, I fell asleep and slept through most of the performance. In spite of my being an unexciting date, he asked me out again. I managed to stay awake that time. A few months later, Curtis asked me to marry him.

It wasn't until after I agreed to marry him that he told me about an unusual vision he'd had weeks before he took me on our first date. In the vision, he knew I was going to be his wife. He told Leigh, who knew all along she and Curtis were not meant to be, plus a few more friends, about his vision and asked them to pray about its meaning. He had never had a profound dream like that before and didn't know what to make of it. After six weeks, one of his friends asked him if he liked me. He said he didn't know. She suggested he take me on a date and find out.

After a short engagement, in 1979, we married and moved to his duplex in University Park, where we tilled up the back yard and planted our first garden. Neither of us had ever gardened before so I can't tell you why we did that. I've often wondered if the desire to dig in the dirt and grow things is something God puts in our hearts. He is a gardener, and we are made in His image.

The only thing I had ever planted before were orange seeds in aluminum pie pans for a science experiment in the fifth grade. I watered those seeds and made sure they had sunshine, but nothing seemed to happen. Soon I became nervous I'd have to take pie pans of dirt to school. Thankfully, on the morning we were to display our projects, small white candy-cane-shaped plants poked out of the black dirt. My experiment was a success! I remember those little sprouts fascinating me. Perhaps because the 1980's were defined by a pervasive fear of nuclear annihilation, I thought we should grow some of our food. Or perhaps it was due to the ongoing debate about whether Christians would be raptured away or have to endure the tribulation that pushed me to try to be self-sustaining. I don't know what propelled us to garden, but together Curtis and I were more inclined to be self-reliant.

Curtis met a scientist in Massachusetts who had developed and patented a leading-edge thermal energy solar system using photovoltaic cells with UV concentrators to increase electricity production in enclosed panels with fans to move the hot air and heat water. We built an off-the-grid lake house using this new technology in the mid 1980's on land we bought in partnership with friends from Dallas. We christened it "Son Up." An underground concrete cellar housed the host of marine batteries that stored our electricity. We installed innovative shower heads that were touted to conserve water but still have the pressure of a regular shower head. We joked we could wash and dry our hair at the same time! The fellow who installed the solar system had little experience with the technology and got a few wires crossed. If you turned on the fan in the living room, the lights in the bedroom turned on instead. It was kind of like playing the memory game.

During this time, a Christian film producer from Los Angeles hired Curtis to do some work for him. We traveled to California for a meeting and while Curtis worked, I watched movies his client had produced. Two of these movies impacted me profoundly. One consisted of interviews with ex-members from a well-known cult about their personal experiences in the group. They realized what they thought was true was a lie and renounced their membership at the cost of being shunned by their friends and families. They claimed they were deceived by leaders who initiated them into secrecy and brainwashed them to trust the leaders unconditionally.

In hindsight, perhaps God was using this movie as a warning of what was to come.

The second film had interviews with several doctors who used to perform abortions. They explained in graphic detail what happened to an unwanted baby during an abortion, and each felt remorse for their actions. Abortion was a hot topic, paralleling the fight to ratify the ERA (Equal Rights for Women). For me, abortion wasn't just a legal or moral battle but was on par with the atrocities my father lived through in World War II. If ever I coaxed him to talk about the war, it seemed to come out disjointed and fragmented. He didn't have the words to describe the horror.

I saw the after-effects of abortion the same way. Young girls were unable to put into words what they felt. They were relieved to no longer be pregnant but unable to process the trauma. They just had to shove their feelings down and move on, carrying around deadweight. Whether it's shame, pain, or fear, these emotions prevented them from being fully alive. In a way, I could relate to these women. Not due to abortion, but because I had secrets about my family that I had never shared with anyone, including Curtis. I didn't have the words to describe the dysfunction in my house while growing up. I couldn't reconcile how my kind, funny, affectionate father worked and played tennis by day and drank too much at night. How very dry martinis turned him into someone I was terrified of. Many times we'd go out to eat and midway through dinner he would start yelling inexplicable things at the waiters. Terrified, I always wanted to hide under the table or just disappear as the entire restaurant went silent in horror. The next day he never gave any explanation. He was his happy self, off to another day at work like nothing had ever happened.

I loved my parents and yet I hated them. I wanted to be brave, courageous and creative like my mother, and yet I felt scared and afraid to try. Confusion and condemnation swirled around in my own heart because I didn't know how to process the things I witnessed growing up. In my own way I felt compassion for girls who felt shame when they found themselves pregnant and alone and scared.

I came back from California with a passion. Possibly the first real direction and purpose I had in my life. I wanted to help young people understand the truth and the effects of abortion. To do that, I began showing the movie that so affected me to thousands of public-school children. There has always been a war waged around unborn babies who can't speak up for themselves, but in the early 1980s, the public schools wanted kids to see the film. The kids sat silent, their attention fixed on the film. Many teachers thanked me for showing it. I prayed every time that the film would make an impact on the kids. That they would think before they acted and if they ended up with an unwanted pregnancy that they'd value life and find healing.

Some friends of ours wanted us to show the movie at our church, but the church leadership refused. The denomination was funding abortions, so the only way we could show the movie was to give equal time to those who were pro-abortion. Curtis and I questioned their decision. If the church didn't stand for the defenseless, what did they stand for? We knew we couldn't stay at a church that supported abortion and offered no other options for those who found themselves in an unplanned pregnancy. Even though we loved our friends dearly, we made the hard decision to leave. I hated the conflict and controversy our decision created among the congregation, but we knew we had made the right decision. Still, that didn't keep us from feeling alone and devastated.

That was the first time in a while I didn't have a church home. It wasn't long before confusion about religion and God and what it meant to be a Christian crept into my mind.

A year after we left our church, a friend called and asked Curtis if he was interested in helping start a new non-denominational church. Four other friends who found themselves either churchless or dissatisfied joined in. After a long search for a pastor, a new church started meeting in a local private school. Soon the building couldn't hold all the people coming to the two services on Sunday, so you can guess what happened next. The five "forward thinking men" (that's what the pastor called the founders) started a building campaign. In the next few years, the church grew to nearly 2,000 members. And we had a big problem. The pastor that everyone loved lied about something to do with money. I couldn't handle any more conflict, so I stayed home most Sundays while the leaders haggled it out with the pastor. Because the pastor refused to leave, Curtis and all the "forward-thinking" men left.

We never thought about not going to church. That's where our friends were and church was supposed to be an anchor in our lives. So far in our short-married life, we'd had two failed attempts.

Once again, we were church homeless.

A Path Divided: Can't Have Both

"Hey Curtis, how are you?" yelled a state representative who happened to be a neighbor.

Thousands of delegates at the 1984 Republican State Convention milled around hobnobbing at the Austin Convention Center. Curtis maybe wanted to run for office someday. He certainly knew a lot of the people at the convention. I couldn't imagine being a politician's wife. I might have to tape my mouth shut for fear I'd help him not get elected. As much as I didn't want to be in politics, I agreed with Curtis that it was our civic duty to help those we thought would represent us well. So, I stuffed envelopes, knocked on doors and made phone calls in hopes the people I liked would get elected. Curtis and I attended as delegates our precinct, district and state conventions.

"You did a great job writing that resolution on parental rights for the platform committee," another passerby yelled above the noise as he patted Curtis on the back and disappeared into the crowd.

Because home schooling wasn't recognized by the state as a school at the time, parents had been prosecuted for truancy. Some had been threatened to have their kids taken away. Parents' rights to home school had become a hot topic at the convention.

After several hours of debate, led by Curtis, the resolution passed. As Curtis made his way back to the convention floor, someone walked up and greeted him by name.

Another man overheard the man say "Curtis," and turned around and asked, "Are you Curtis Brown?" Curtis responded, "Yes I am." The stranger continued, "I heard you wrote the resolution on parental rights and homeschooling." "Yes, I did," Curtis responded. "My name is Howard Wheeler. I just wanted to thank you for writing it. Our church has been harassed by the state."

Howard, a tall, large man with an imposing deep voice, belonged to Emmaus Christian Fellowship, later renamed Homestead Heritage. Meeting him was the beginning of our entry there. Curtis and Howard talked for an hour and a half and agreed to stay in touch.

Over the coming months Howard told us about his community, which had started on East 14th Street "in Hell's Kitchen" in Manhattan. He referred to his leader as Brother Blair, a man who had sacrificed everything for God.

We were attracted to the lifestyle he painted of his community. He portrayed a picture of a simple life where the members gardened and loved each other. It sounded like our dream come true. We wanted our children to grow up in a safe place with diverse, like-minded people who cared for the elderly, single moms, and the sick. The more Howard talked, the more Curtis and I thought of our current situation. We longed for a church home, for a community. Howard and Curtis got along well. They even began meeting with Christian political leaders around the state to discuss current issues like homeschooling. Curtis was excited by the idea that he could help Howard's small community. It felt good to be needed.

At first, the church group seemed unusual, but we slowly warmed up to them. We went so far as convincing ourselves they were a picture of what the church was supposed to look like. The few members lived near each other, homeschooled, ate food from their gardens, orchards, and livestock. They helped one another when they were sick or after a home birth and provided for those who lacked anything. After the chaotic church upheavals we had witnessed, this new community looked so compelling. As though it was the answer to all the confusion and violence in the world. Everything Howard advocated jived with what we wanted in life. In some ways it reminded me of my wonderland experience growing up in Chickasaw Gardens. And I wanted that experience for my kids.

Curtis and I thought the cost of joining Homestead would be worth it. We knew that we'd be giving up everything we knew and valued from the past. Somehow, we convinced ourselves this group was where we belonged. For years in fact, we thought living there was God's will for us.

Five years passed from the time we met Howard and the others at Homestead until we joined. By then our minds and belief systems had already succumbed, unbeknownst to us, to reprogramming under the guise of "moving into the full revelation of God" while living a simple life among our "new faithful family." Our trust in God and those we had known and loved was slowly transferred to people we really didn't know. But we didn't know any of that at the time. What we did know was that we wanted to be on this adventure with a church that was living "like the first century church." I knew I wanted to wholeheartedly trust God with everything. I knew I had had an easy life and something in me wanted to step out into the deep and completely trust Him, even if it was hard. Giving up everything for Him seemed like the right way to show Him that I trusted Him.

Little did we know we were being scammed. God knew and tried to warn us, but just as Blair, the founder, had needs in him that caused him to scam others, we had needs that allowed ourselves to be scammed. Not long ago my computer announced out loud in a human voice that it had been hacked. I was about ten minutes into the "solution" when I realized it was a very clever scam - one that I thought I'd never fall for! In life, people get scammed in jobs, in marriages, relationships, churches;

the list goes on and on. We get scammed because we get caught off guard, and we put our hope in the wrong things. Our souls are sick, and we seek solace in the wrong places. We're untethered to the Truth. Hope deferred makes the heart sick. Sometimes some of us lose our way.

For a while after we met Howard we lived in Dallas and spent weekends with friends at Son Up, our lake house in east Texas. I was still an active member of the Dallas Junior League. I wore the latest fashions from Mam'selle, played tennis, jogged, and had a new haircut every six weeks. But on the inside, we felt at times unanchored, and didn't belong anywhere. We were ripe for the bait that was about to be offered.

Setting Up a Generation

After the Second World War and into the fifties and sixties, my parents, along with all my friends' parents, were hell-bent on making a lot of money, so we didn't see that much of them. They didn't seem to notice what we were doing. As long as we weren't in jail, they were happy. They sent us off to school all year and camp all summer. My mother didn't have time to take me to driver's ed, so she let me drive myself to the classes that were held next door to the police station. Never mind I didn't have a driver's license and the reason I was going was to learn how to drive.

I don't remember ever really getting any advice from my mother. If she was around, I could get her to sign a note for school. If not, she said I could forge her name. One thing she did teach me was writing —and plagiarizing—by having me copy book reviews from the New York Times.

In the 80's many in my generation swung in the opposite direction of our parents and hovered over our children. We seemed hell-bent on protecting them from all the evil in the world.

In hindsight I think the fear of losing our kids to the evil of the 1980's world was the catalyst for the expansion of the home-schooling movement. Instead of trusting our kids with others, we thought we would be their best teachers. I didn't think that about myself. I thought I'd be a terrible teacher. But all the homeschooling books were saying, "Who could teach better than the parents?" Nuclear bombs might blow the world up at the touch of a button. Our children needed a strong foundation so they could withstand the influence of atheist, communist professors that taught on college campuses. We no longer assumed our kids would go to college. It was now, "If they go to college." Home schoolers joined forces and formed support groups, political action groups, and legal defense funds. When we lived in Dallas, our older kids would not dare be caught outside during school hours for fear we'd be hauled off to jail.

The Radical Shift Begins

Our new friend, Howard, started coming to Dallas more frequently. He spoke about homeschooling on a popular radio program aired from Dallas, and he taught what we assumed to be Bible studies to potential members of his group in Ft. Worth. He stayed with us on many occasions, and the more our church life fell apart, the more we came to identify with his way of thinking. One week, he invited us to what he called a Friday night meeting. A few families from Waco had joined the Fellowship, and one couple hosted a small home group at their farm on the north side of Waco. They all drove to Austin on Sundays to meet with the entire congregation for Sunday meetings. I looked forward to the meeting as I got our four kids ready to go. Our oldest was seven and the youngest was a baby. I didn't know what to expect, but with all Howard had told us, it was sure to be different from any church experience we'd ever had. I wore my long chambray jumper with the white Laura Ashley puff sleeve blouse. I was shocked to find the meeting full of women with buns and men dressed in jeans and mostly plaid shirts sitting next to little girls with tidy braids hanging down their backs and clean-cut boys dressed in plaid shirts. Like little replicas of their parents. The owner of the house and his wife greeted us at the door. All eyes felt fixed on us. I took a deep breath and entered the room with a little trepidation. Our host proceeded to the front of the room and sat by a lady holding a guitar in her lap. He slung a guitar over his shoulder as we were escorted to our seats at the front of the room. I hoped the kids would go to sleep since the meeting started at eight o'clock which was close to their bedtime. I closed my eyes like everyone else as a low moaning sound spread across the room. It grew louder and louder until everyone in the room joined in. I couldn't make out any words, but I remember thinking, "This must be what it's like at the Wailing Wall in Jerusalem."

After the two-hour meeting, our hosts invited us to have some snacks and led us to the front of the line. There was popcorn and carob-no-bakes and desserts made with whole wheat and honey. We drank tea sweetened with honey that made me thirsty on the late drive home that night. The meeting was different from anything I had ever attended. Many people had shared a Scripture or a word they felt was from the Lord. The musicians sang with all their hearts. The people seemed sincere in their faith, and we felt welcomed, included and flattered by all the fuss they made over us.

That was the first of many Friday night meetings we attended where we heard about the humble beginnings of the group and how Blair and his wife had given up everything and moved to New York City to start a mission church there. It was all so opposite of us starting a church with one committee that branched off into a search committee to look for a pastor. The way they described how the Fellowship started made sense and seemed to work organically. It was like what we thought it might have been like in the first century church.

The love the people poured out on us made us feel more and more at home in the group. Over time we accepted the dress and ladies' uncut hair and unusual style of corporate worship where everyone shouted "Hallelujah" simultaneously and continuously. We assumed the group was built on the same truth as the other churches we had belonged to. Once when Howard came to our house for one of his visits, he spent an inordinate amount of time reading the titles of the books on our bookshelves. He exclaimed authoritatively, "You have a lot of books about Abraham Lincoln!" We stopped and listened as he launched into a diatribe against who we thought was an American hero. He quoted authors who condemned Lincoln as eccentric, selfish, and purposely initiated and perpetuated the Civil War to make a name for himself. When he finally finished talking, I was stunned and almost embarrassed that I could possibly think Abraham Lincoln was an American hero. I wondered what we were supposed to teach our kids. Howard said Brother Blair was working on history books for kids that would tell the truth. Still feeling inadequate in my homeschooling abilities, that sounded good to me.

It felt like we had passed a test when Howard called and asked us if we wanted to attend our first "church wide" meeting. It would be on New Year's Eve at night with the whole group, not just the small Friday night meetings we'd started attending in Waco on a fairly regular basis. They met in a metal warehouse in the country southeast of Austin. The building had been the Black Hat Saloon. Howard didn't call it a church service. He always called the gatherings "meetings." He said we'd sing in the New Year. I was thrilled and excited.

Maybe it would be a whole band and not just one or two people playing a guitar. To hear two or three hundred people loudly praying simultaneously like they do must be deafening and thrilling. I'll have to prepare the kids. Could they sit still and stay quiet like the Fellowship kids did at the Friday night meetings? I doubt it. Surely the members would understand since we're new at all this. Now, what to wear? Curtis will easily fit in among the men. I'll have to wear the same blue chambray jumper with the big mix matched enamel buttons. The kids at the Friday night meetings seemed enamored with those buttons. The cute little girls with the tidy braids loved to touch them. The clean-cut little boys in jeans and plaid shirts stood off to the side and stared. It is the only long dress I have, and I don't want to stick out any more than I already do.

I looked at myself with despair. My hair was too short to braid or put in a bun. I decided to forgo wearing makeup and jewelry, and hoped they didn't notice the nail polish. I paced my bedroom floor in shorts and a tee shirt worrying about fitting in with people I didn't even know. I'd be the only odd one in a large group where they all looked alike. And they seemed genuinely happy and peaceful. Like they'd given up all the fads and fashions for a simpler life that gave them rest. It felt like they belonged.

We'd met Brother Blair on many occasions by then but had never heard him preach. This New Year's gathering would be our first time.

The other times we had met him, he seemed like a kindhearted jolly man who could speak with authority, but that night there was nothing jolly about him. The meeting itself was nothing remotely like a singalong. After one song, Brother Blair read a Scripture about Hell and someone else popped up in the audience and yelled out that someone was going to suffer terrible circumstances and sat down. Much groaning and wailing ensued and then the room became silent. I didn't know what we were waiting for, but it seemed forever before someone made a sound. To my shock the man sitting behind me bounded out of his seat and as he jerked both arms into the air, he accidentally hit me in the head. He cried out that he had sinned. He begged for forgiveness for being such a reproach on the "body." I sat riveted to my seat staring at the floor. No one wanted to go through what that poor person was going through. I wondered what sin he had committed and decided it must have been really bad. After the man's confession the mood became lighter. Someone sang an upbeat song. As soon as the meeting was over

Howard dashed over to us and said jokingly with his confident smile, "How's that for singing in the New Year? You just never know what the Lord might do in one of our meetings."

The more accepted we felt, the more we accepted the unusual things we witnessed. Howard always had a logical explanation for everything we questioned, even when Brother Blair railed against Abraham Lincoln on many occasions from the pulpit. Was Brother Blair admitting he favored slavery or was I misconstruing what he was saying? His message seemed too vague for me to outright question him. At the time, it all kind of made sense and the newness of it kept us holding on.

Giving it All to God

Raising four small children who all needed my attention kept me constantly on the go, but after that first New Year's Eve meeting, I rarely had time to think. I found myself either packing to drive to Waco for a Friday night meeting and then on to Austin for a Sunday meeting or unpacking from the weekend away. Many Sunday nights we arrived home at one or two in the morning and had to haul four soundly sleeping kids up a long flight of stairs to their beds. I don't think they ever brushed their teeth on the weekends.

Later on, Brother Howard started a teaching series on Friday nights and spent more time at our house in Dallas. There were other families from the area interested in joining the Fellowship, (the informal name everyone called the group back then), so sometimes we had around sixty people crammed into our living room. That meant I spent the little energy I had getting ready for company and cooking for the families that drove up from Austin and Waco for the meetings. My mother came to one of the meetings at my house. She sat on the front row in a white short dress and white shiny hose. I wore a long white dress. The more questions my mother asked, the hotter my face felt. I picked up my baby and paced in the back of the room to keep from having a complete nervous breakdown.

Howard finally said, "Bettye, you can be quiet now," and that made her even madder, if that was possible. She hated Howard and everything that was taking us away from her. I felt paralyzed. I wanted to please her but felt this was God's will for us. I also felt that by joining the group I'd break free from her control. In my heart I felt I owed her so much, but I also resented her and felt I was yanking myself free from a stranglehold. She wasn't going to back down. She didn't trust Howard any more than she could throw him and told me flat out, "He's a liar."

When Curtis and I returned to Memphis after our honeymoon to pack my car and drive to Dallas, Mama tried to convince Curtis to keep the Tennessee license plates on my car. She said it would save money. Curtis argued, "I could be disbarred for doing that. That's a crime." Undeterred she glared at Curtis and stomped off like a sore loser. Later when she realized Curtis took great care of his family and had a successful career ahead of him, she came to love and trust him and frequently sought his counsel. Not so with Brother Howard and Brother Blair. She reminded me from time to time that, "You can't trust a fat preacher."

Howard called on Curtis's legal expertise constantly. He'd call the house looking for Curtis and I'd feel compelled to track him down wherever he might be at the time. In 1989 we sold our house in Dallas and moved to Son Up, our remote lake house in east Texas. The year we lived at Son Up Curtis and Howard talked so much our phone bill was $12,000.00!! It seemed the Fellowship faced crisis after crisis. Howard knew Curtis loved to help people and he knew Curtis would take his calls no matter what he was doing. Curtis had legal research skills the Fellowship needed, even though he knew little about the topics Howard had him research. Curtis's experience was in income tax planning for large companies and estate planning for high-net-worth individuals. No one in the Fellowship had much of any net worth. Curtis started out researching things like horse insurance and buying and installing mobile homes, as that's what almost everyone lived in. He was asked to study laws about home births including birth certificates. He delved into exemptions concerning vaccinations, sales tax exemptions, social security exemption for ministers, incorporating churches, and jury service. Curtis spent a lot of time learning about these issues as a courtesy. He is a rule follower and wanted to help them comply with the law. Howard said they would pay him when they could, but they didn't have any money. Curtis ended up doing legal work for thirty years and was never paid a penny. Howard would always, in his way, laugh it off that Curtis's specialty was "pro bono."

One night Howard called Curtis and said a member was on his way to Dallas with a paper he wanted us to read. He thought we might be ready to join. It had been almost five years since we had met the Fellowship. I still wore makeup and jeans and cut my hair but felt like I was living a double life. Joining would be the end of my life as I knew it, but I loved the meetings and what I thought was the presence of God. I had crossed a line and felt like there was no turning back. Curtis was very involved helping them out in the legal arena and I loved the way the people seemed to care for one another. Even if it was from a distance. I wanted the kids to have good friends and grow up in a safe environment. Most of all I wanted to trust God. We had convinced ourselves that He had led us to this place.

The people in Homestead were from varied backgrounds. Some had been hippies whose families were part of the Mafia in New York. Some were transformed drug addicts and others were craftsmen. One man was from Beverly Hills, California, and his parents were on the board that voted on the Academy Awards. Quite a few were Jewish and others were from every faith background imaginable. They even had four Israelis who were members.

Still, voices inside our heads said this was a radical decision. Our friends and family questioned the sincerity of the group. Why did they change their name so much? They were called "Voice in the Wilderness" in New York? Why were they first called "Emmaus Christian Fellowship" in Texas but changed the name to "Koinonia Communities"? What did that even mean? And later to "Heritage Ministries." Why did they leave

Colorado and their beautiful ranch there? Our parents were concerned about the lifestyle. Did we really want to commit to homeschool? They feared we'd never allow their grandkids to go to college. They wanted their grandkids to get a college education more than anything. One of my mother's close friends told her the people in the Fellowship looked like Holy Rollers. Trying to get some answers for my parents, I asked Howard if they were from a Pentecostal background. Howard said they were not, but were from all different backgrounds. My mother especially felt the people were sweet but a lot like dumb, blind sheep who were told what to do. The women she said were oppressed and looked miserable and overworked and bedraggled. Why would I want to look like that and give up having my own opinion? Some feared we'd live without modern conveniences, and I'd die of exhaustion. One dear friend from college took me to lunch one day and asked, "Does it have to be this way? Do you have to separate yourselves from all of us to be a part of the Fellowship? Aren't we all a part of the Body of Christ?"

Howard and the other leaders persuaded us that doing the Lord's will was never easy. Every time we questioned why they held a certain belief, they had an answer they gave authoritatively. They quoted *John 7:17(NIV), Anyone who chooses to do the will of God will find out whether my teaching comes from God or whether I speak on my own,* frequently and taught that if you have made up your mind to follow the Lord, you would know their teaching was from God. When I asked why they rejected the Trinity, Howard said they didn't believe in three gods!

Well, I didn't believe in three gods either, so I believed he was right, even though my heart still didn't quite understand. Usually, Howard or another leader responded to my questions with, "What did you feel at the meeting you went to?" or "Didn't you feel loved at the fellowship the other night?" Little did we know we were learning to overrule our own minds and hearts and rely on the feelings we had during emotionally charged times together. We trusted them and believed what they told us was the truth. We wanted more of God, and the Fellowship seemed to offer everything we wanted for our kids and our lives. The churches we had joined in Dallas had serious problems, so it seemed God was opening a door for us to join a church with harmony among the members. We were excited but also scared because it seemed so permanent. It was our last effort at finding a church home.

We were baptized on a Sunday in April 1989 in Austin in a concrete trough. We had driven to Austin the night before. The closer we got to Austin, the slower Curtis drove. Once we reached the city limits he asked me, "Do you want to drive around a while?" I squinted up my eyes and shook my head, "No."

We'd been in the car with four little kids for four hours and he wanted to stall. He was taking deep breaths and sighing a lot. I, on the other hand, wanted to get it over with. Curits drove slower and slower while we listened to a Bach concerto until we finally got to the house we were staying at. Howard and other members greeted us, and Curtis asked them if they wanted to listen to some Bach. "What on earth!" I thought. He wants to back out and I'm all in! At other times it was the other way around. Looking back, I realize we rarely were on the same page as far as joining went.

We both had been baptized when we were younger, but getting rebaptized was a requirement to join. Anyone who had been baptized as a "Trinitarian" was required to be rebaptized. Even elderly grandparents who had taught Bible studies and ministered in nursing homes for years were required to be initiated into the group by being rebaptized "in Jesus's name only." It was a beautiful day and when I came out of the water, I looked around at all these people I didn't know who were my family now. I must have hugged hundreds of strangers that day. The weight of what Curtis was leading his family into fell on him hard. I had never seen him cry before; he was overcome with emotion as he gave his life to an unknown. They had taught us a new song that said, *"We left our kinfolk gladly, we bid this world goodbye..."* so we did just that. We separated ourselves from all we had ever known to join ourselves to these people we didn't really know at all.

We were looking for a place to belong and for more of God. We were at a crossroads in life, dealing with confusing events surrounding the church, and we were vulnerable and looking for community. I thought the Fellowship looked like the first century church where it seemed everyone's gifts were allowed to flourish. I thought this was the way the Body of Christ was supposed to work. And we were lucky enough to have found it. What we did not know was that we were allowing ourselves to be lured into Homestead and into a bondage of fear.

We were being homogenized.

Trying to Please and Hitting a Wall

We joked that our fifth child would be an astronaut because she seemed to always be buckled up in her car seat. At the drop of a hat, we'd jump in the car with all of the kids and drive to Austin to a special meeting or if we were invited to a function with Blair and his wife. Only the group leaders or elders close to Brother Blair were invited to some of those gatherings. On a few occasions we ate at a Chinese restaurant and on the long drive home our fifth, the future astronaut, would complain, "I've got MSG!" meaning she was car sick. She must have heard us talking about MSG being an ingredient in the food we had eaten, and she associated it with car sickness.

We were flattered to be among the group Blair spent time with, and Regina, Blair's wife, became my good friend. She wasn't the kind of friend I could just call any time I wanted to. After all she was Blair's wife and very busy being at his beck and call. I put her on a pedestal and learned early on to treat her with the highest respect. Over the years I wrote her dozens of sweet cards and would deliberate at length about what to get her for her birthday. I felt thrilled to be called her good friend and thought we'd be that way forever. Whenever she called me with a question, no matter what I was doing I'd take her call and snap my fingers at my kids to keep them quiet. I didn't want to be a "burden" to her, as we called it, by having "out of it" children.

At the fellowships we attended, the men repeated funny stories of the groups' unusual beginnings, a band of older kids entertained us with music, and the food was always delicious. We were even allowed to be at fellowships with important potential new members whose turn it was to enjoy all the attention. Frequently Blair shared about frightening things happening in the world and everyone sat transfixed on his every word. They then responded with thanksgiving for him as a leader, and that he was so close to God that he created an *ark* where they were safe as members of the Fellowship.

Somehow my children learned to read despite all the time I spent preparing for the busy weekends that included lengthy meetings, showers, anniversary parties, birthday parties, and the occasional wedding. I did have a habit of reading out loud to my kids. And we had plenty of time to read on the many road trips to Austin. I began buying things to fill up a present box, so I'd have a present on hand for the frequent occasions. Trying to fit in and please everyone spurred me to attempt to reform my children into kids like those in *David and Susan and the Little Green House* where the children never said a cross word to each other. If one fell down, the other wiped away the other's tears. That had never happened at my house. We had a house full of real kids.

The leaders attributed the clean-cut, docile, and happy congregation to the absence of competition and the insistence on cooperation. The emphasis on perfection led to the goal of excellence in all things. The leaders repeated certain Scriptures: *Whatever you do, do it with all of your heart. Strive for perfection! Believe that you will obtain it, and you will obtain it. All things are possible to him who believes. Do your work wholeheartedly as unto the Lord.* These verses applied to everything from keeping house to child training to crafts and running a business. The reputation of the Fellowship depended on it, and I spent decades trying to shift myself and my family into being perfect. For the sake of the Fellowship.

We attended meetings where Blair sternly warned his followers not to miss God's timing. It was as though everything was a now or never event. My grandmother's biggest fear had been that God would pass her by. Now, the leaders preached that God was passing by. Alarmed, I wondered if He would wait for me. Whenever someone was called out publicly in a meeting, I nervously questioned if I was the one God was pointing His finger at. If I tried my best but failed to keep my parents happy when I was little, I tended to blame myself. Now, within the Fellowship, I wanted to be perfect for God--the One who saved me, and those He had put "over me," but each time I failed I became more fearful and anxious.

Most of the meetings we attended consisted of members confessing failures and repenting and recommitting themselves to the Fellowship. If no one fessed up, the tension built up in the room as the leaders incriminated someone by implying doom was just about to fall on whoever had blown it. They did this by reading a familiar Scripture like the one about the rich young ruler who failed to give everything up and walked away sad. Or they boomed that Jesus was walking along the beach and commanding, "Follow Me." A leader might request a song that had been revised for the occasion like, "There can be miracles if only you believe..."

I'm not sure how everyone else was feeling during those stressful meetings, but I sat there anxiously wondering what I possibly could have done. When I found out it was someone else, I always sighed with relief. I was off the hook until the next meeting. I hoped I would never fall as far as that poor soul.

The longing for a tight-knit community slowly overruled our questions and our family and friends' concerns. An exchange of our true selves for the people we needed to be to fit in began to slowly take place. It went like this: "I give up my personality so that you'll be my friends for life and our kids will be safe and we'll live happily ever after."

In our desire to give everything to God, we sold most everything and gave it to the Fellowship. To us this was the modern-day equivalent of selling everything and laying it at the apostles' feet like they did in the book of Acts. Most of the members were poor, and we wanted to be able to help those who needed it. We believed that's what God wanted us to do, and I knew I didn't deserve all I had been given. I was spoiled after all. But we had doubts about our donation when Curtis found out that all our money was going to pay off the Fellowship's large debt. Because they were in default, creditors were set to seize Rehoboth Ranch, the 1500-acre ranch where Blair and Regina lived in Colorado, about an hour and a half away from most of the members of the church. Curtis was livid. He voiced his concerns clearly, and the next thing we knew, Howard was at our house in Dallas trying to convince us that it wasn't as bad as we thought it was. He had a powerful gift of persuasion and was the spokesman for the group. He talked and didn't let you argue with whatever he said. This time Curtis was arguing though. He wanted to help the group progress, not just cover up their irresponsible decisions. They clearly knew nothing about business or money, except how to waste it. While Curtis spoke his mind to Howard, I sat on the couch smocking a dress for my daughter and hating all the conflict. I don't remember how, but Howard once again won, and we committed to press on. This time with no money. We had cut off the lifeboat. We had no back door or escape route. There was no turning back.

We convinced ourselves that this was what the church in the book of Acts looked like.

There was not a needy person among them, for as many as were owners of lands or houses sold them and brought the proceeds of what was sold and laid it at the apostles' feet, and it was distributed to each as any had need. Acts 4:34-35 (ESV)

Putting our Dreams into Practice

After we gave the Fellowship all our other assets, we gave them the proceeds from the sale of our house in University Park to buy a 350-acre farm as well as top of the line mobile homes for Blair and Howard to live in. Curtis earned enough money over the next two years to build a log house on the farm we had bought for them. The land was called Brazos de Dios, as it bordered the Brazos River north of Waco, Texas. Then we paid rent to live "on the Land" as they commonly called the community compound. But we were happy. We were living our dream on a beautiful farm with like-minded neighbors. Immediately we bought turkeys, chickens, and goats. What we didn't do first was make sure we had some way to confine them all. The kids constructed ramshackle makeshift coops and corrals. We learned quickly that goats are escape artists who soon ate all of our neighbors' landscaping.

I thought living "on the Land" would make homeschooling a breeze because all the moms were doing the same thing. I had been home schooling for a few years by then and never felt like I was doing a good job. I anticipated home schooling in the Fellowship would be like joining an organized support group where we used the same curriculum and helped each other. Brother Blair hadn't sanctioned much curriculum at the time but assured us that more was forthcoming. He was adamant that we steer away from teaching any history because only he knew the "correct" version. During those years, there wasn't much homeschooling curriculum on the market so we did the best we could with what we could round up. Sister Regina said she and Blair had carefully edited kids' books that she let her kids read but she never shared any suggestions. On a few occasions, when one of my kids told one of her kids they had read a certain book, I'd get a call reprimanding me for not having the wisdom to know that book was "out of it!" One Sunday church wide meeting was devoted to reprimanding someone in the congregation for allowing their child to read a classic. They didn't mention the title of the book, so I had no idea the meeting was directed at me. I had not responded in the meeting by standing up and humbling myself by repenting in front of the congregation for being a bad example. It was expedient for the leaders to use one person's mistake as a public example. Our son had read the classic, *Les Misérables.* That displeased Blair. He was hoping that my testimony before the congregation would send a message to the entire group; the classics were considered banned books. In this case as happened sometimes, I failed to see that Blair's displeasure was directed at me, so I had to have a separate "ministry session" with Howard so I wouldn't make that mistake again. Another time a Homeschool advisor made the mistake of suggesting the book "The Trapp Family Singers," (the book the movie *The Sound of Music* was based on) as a "safe" book for our kids to read. I loved that book and was thrilled to read it out loud to my kids. No sooner had we started the book when we all heard from Sister Regina to not read that book because it encouraged wanderlust in our kids. As I recall the Trapp family was fleeing the Nazis and lost everything they had. I failed at picking up any hint of wanderlust in the book, but stopped reading it out loud to my kids in order to stay in compliance with the "patterns" and Sister Regina. In the Fellowship, all classics were off limits, and books the "world" liked were not "us." In the end, it didn't matter. We had very little time for school those early years.

The older kids took turns milking the community cows in the early mornings and evenings. We were instructed to leave the fresh milk on the front shelves for the Adams family. In case the kids forgot, someone taped a sign to the shelf in the walk-in cooler that stated in bold letters, "For the Adamses only." The members whose kids did the milking were to take the oldest milk on the back row for their families. Oftentimes the milk my kids brought home tasted like a cow smells. In between milking they tended our garden, collected the eggs, and took care of all our many animals.

I loved the wholesome life the kids spent outdoors caring for animals and the land. They learned crafts and played musical instruments. Learning skills fostered responsibility and confidence. I, on the other hand, spent time sorting out "bad" things my kids had supposedly said to someone else's kids, or what someone else's kid had said to mine, spending countless hours on the phone with ministers. Nothing seemed to ever get resolved or made right, but eventually there would be another issue to address so we just moved on.

When I wasn't putting out fires about kids' behavior, I was spending untold hours getting ready for the many visitors who passed through the farm. In addition to working full time for clients outside the Fellowship, Curtis spent hours working on legal issues for the Fellowship and was rarely home. His aggravation with the kids grew with each tedious phone call from Howard and my stress level rose daily. Slowly, I found myself loving the kids less and yelling more. My "place" became cooking and cleaning, gardening, teaching and training our now six kids. I rarely washed my face and never used conditioner on my hair. I was either pregnant or nursing a baby and felt like crying a lot. Other moms confessed the same thing, and those confessions would result in their getting "ministered to" for not having enough faith and not sacrificing enough. I learned from their "mistakes" and never confessed my feelings of overwhelm. Instead, I soldiered on in silence. Looking back, I managed to rally whenever we were allowed to sit at the table with Brother Blair and Sister Regina at a birthday or anniversary fellowship.

This was a sort of reward for our sacrifice and seemed to motivate me to keep trying to please.

Meetings became the focus of our week that everything else revolved around. To miss a meeting might mean "missing out" with God, so unless one of the kids was sick, we went. We had a prayer meeting every Tuesday night, a youth meeting on Wednesday night, a Friday night group meeting that visitors were allowed to attend and the big members-only Sunday meeting that might last three or four hours. Brother Blair shared his big dreams of showing the world how our community was nothing like any other on the earth. He frequently retold the story of the community's beginnings in New York City in Hell's Kitchen. Despite the hardships of our new lifestyle, we felt like we were part of the continuing narrative, our lives merging with those first "pioneers." Blair often called us all "Wisdom's Children" (the title of one of Brother Blair's early books) if we put into practice his ideas, --ideas he claimed were based on the Bible. Many times, we heard the message that all our problems would be solved if we committed our lives to the big picture. This idea convinced me to stuff away any grievance or question and join in wholeheartedly. We had a lot to live up to. The pressure was on. There was no time to ponder my questions.

Each year Brother Blair announced his yearly project which was usually a new building to house a craft, like pottery or fibrecrafts. These projects took more of the kids' time because the boys were expected to help build the buildings and the girls were required to stay up all hours making snacks for the work crews. Blair wanted to make sure we put out a good image to the community so no one would accuse us of being a cult. The image of wholesomeness and of a time gone by were paramount. The grand finale testimony at most meetings was given by Brother Howard who affirmed Brother Blair's message of either doom and gloom and the soon shutting of the doors of the ark, or a prophetic word that proclaimed something big "was just around the corner."

Part Two

The Language We Learned

Homestead, like other cults, teaches its members a certain vocabulary exclusively their own. The language we learned there had meaning only among the group.

> I found this explanation of how language loading works: "A cultic group often uses its own complex vocabulary. Words carry with them entire packages of implications, emotions, metaphors, and even past experiences. They invent new words and phrases that carry with them much more complicated understandings, or they manipulate existing words to change their meanings subtly or dramatically. Loaded language serves several purposes:

1. Relabels or redefines meanings.
2. Shuts down critical thinking ability.
3. Further isolates the group making it difficult to communicate with outsiders.

> "Concepts can be relabeled with emotionally charged words which carry preconceived notions. These can be used to make something seem automatically positive and

> impossible to argue against, or inherently negative and impossible to argue for."[1]

This new language had a certain meaning when we interacted with one another, almost like a secret code that only we knew the meaning of. I probably said, "I'm going through it" a thousand times meaning I was in trouble for saying the wrong thing or wearing the wrong thing or any number of infractions that I was made to feel guilty of.

At times Blair would light-heartedly say in a meeting that our brains were being washed, like it was a good thing. He referred to the verse in Ephesians 5:26, and because our brains had been rewired to trust the founder who, he repeatedly reminded us, had sacrificed so much for us, we believed he would never do us any harm. He even published a book on mind control to validate himself and prove that he did not practice brainwashing and his group was not just another cult. I think he recalled that book, meaning we had to turn it back in after we had bought it, as he did others when he realized it wasn't going to help his image. That book was an explanation of how brainwashing works, and it was like him saying, "I'm not guilty of this!" That might make more astute people question why he needed to refute his actions if nobody was questioning him. He discouraged us from reading any books, even Christian books, unless he approved them. I remember only a few obscure books that he approved in thirty years. He did require us to read the many books he wrote, and rewrote. Those books, along with mandatory, usually emotionally charged, meetings where he redefined words and Scriptures

---

1. https://www.recoveringagency.com/articles/the-methods-of-thought-reform/loading-the-language/ Assessed 09/21/2023

in an effort to teach us a new language, as he called it, helped all of us stay within the Homestead language boundaries.

I remember when Curtis was a minister and a couple wanted to travel out of state to see their three children and grandchildren. Another minister warned Curtis to discourage them from visiting their family for more than a few days because they would "lose their language." This was another indication that language at Homestead was a way to isolate, control, and manipulate the members.

Thou Shalt Not

Honor, flanked by *Order*, was the topic of choice when we first joined and it remained the underpinning of life at Homestead until we left. These two teachings were the *form*, as Blair called it, that *held the conten*t that informed us. The content included his decisions that controlled everything about our lives. He earned our trust by toggling between his kind and funny, sometimes winsome way, that warmed our hearts toward him, interspersed with a temper that scared us to death. Strangely we kept trusting him. Without realizing it, he became God to us. As time went on living in the Fellowship, we unknowingly quit trusting the real God and instead transferred our trust to a human man who was no better than anyone else. Blair said in a meeting that if he had one final message to preach it would be on "order." He and his leadership were the *order,* and we had to *honor* the *order* to survive. This system of honor and order culminated in the *patterns of God* that we were to follow. That's how he implemented this system of control and measured our righteousness.

Order + honor = patterns. That was our life.

The patterns of God regulated our clothing, hair, food, birthing practices, lifestyle, education, entertainment, boy/girl relationships, and family structure. I should clarify that these patterns were mostly unwritten and subject to change over the years, even though he convinced us they were on par with the Ten Commandments that never change. The word "rule" can be substituted for the word "pattern" if that helps you understand what a pattern was at Homestead.

I recall a time when I was still a member, but after I realized Homestead was just another cult, Blair's son, Aber, who was also a leader, loudly proclaimed four times at a communion service, "The order *is* Christ," and formed the shape of a pyramid with his hands. He made it clear that his father sat at the tippy top of this order, his handpicked delegatees under him, and all the rest of us at the bottom. He clearly proclaimed that his father, Blair Adams, who created this "order," was Christ, though without saying it outright. With my eyes no longer veiled, I sat there thinking, "Does that mean what I think he's saying?"

I looked around, but no one questioned his words. The realization that I had exchanged my faith in Jesus for faith in a man sank deep into me. Remorse gripped my heart while I grappled with the truth that I too had been living in fear, too afraid of the consequences to challenge the false teaching.

Their supreme teaching was that Homestead was the only "fitly framed" church in the world because this "order of perfection" (the title of one of Blair's books) set Homestead apart from all other churches in the world. The order was Blair. Honor was our devotion to him, and if a member disagreed with the order, he or she would be disciplined. Constant fear of upsetting the order of the apple cart kept us obeying the unwritten patterns that we were told were not rules. The *Order* did not want Homestead to be thought of as a rules-based group. That would be legalistic.

'Tis a Gift to be Simple

"Tis a gift to be simple, tis a gift to be free." ("Simple Gifts" written by Elder Joseph Brackett, 1848)

This was the theme song frequently played at meetings when we joined Homestead. It made me think of the simple life. A life away from the bustling crowds where we were free from frivolous endeavors and controversies. Free from politics and competition and engaging culture. All we had to do was reject and criticize anything outside of Homestead. It sounded wholesome. It was part of the reason I wanted to join. But life at Homestead was anything but simple or free.

Tattling: an unspoken pattern

We had just recently joined when a minister's wife called to ask me why I had questioned Brother Blair's harsh public rebuke at the first meeting we went to. I tried to think back to what I had said. After thinking for a while, I remembered asking her what the man had done to deserve that? She had responded by saying, "Brother Blair knew what was best for him. He knows what's right."

She told me Brother Howard said I had dishonored Brother Blair. I, my mouth not yet under control, responded with, "Well, he's lying. I didn't say anything to dishonor him!"

The next thing I knew, Brother Howard called Curtis and explained in no uncertain terms what I had done wrong. I had dishonored Brother Blair by questioning his authority, and unbeknownst to me, I committed a double whammy by accusing his right-hand man of being a liar. Between all the phone calls and discussions my head was spinning, but I soon got the picture: I needed to watch what I said. Brother Howard gave me this advice, "There are some things you can tell Curtis. There are some things you can tell a sister. And there are some things you should only tell God." He left it up to me to discern what to do with that advice.

There was so much to learn about this honor business. The advice I gave to myself was, "I need to keep my big mouth shut!" And so, I became a little more discerning as to what would keep those in authority happy and a little more calculating when I communicated with members. I had a lively personality at the time and spoke my mind usually without thinking first. Curtis was "ministered" to by Brother Howard to encourage me to exhibit a quiet and gentle spirit and that my "place" was to serve him. Submission was a hot topic in the American church generally back then, but has always been a practiced doctrine at Homestead. The roles and "place" of women and men were clearly delineated. Being easily condemned and wanting to please, I complied. Rather piecemeal over the first years, I'd stuff a little of myself into an imaginary box that I picture now as at the bottom of my heart. A carefully crafted new self emerged on the outside for all to see the change in me. The newer, submissive me. Over the years I could predict what would happen to new members if the wife was outspoken, opinionated, or seemed unsubmissive to her husband. She became a quiet, less joyful person, fearful she might "get out of her place." We heard much persuasive teaching on finding our place in this ark Brother Blair had erected with his amazing foresight and wisdom. I became a little less joyful one conversation and ministry session at a time.

When we joined Homestead, we envisioned having close relationships where we could share our hearts and work through conflicts in a mature way. Instead, I lived in constant fear of "being in trouble."

To maintain the façade of upholding *the glory of God*, members were compelled to snitch (or tattle) on their own children, spouse, brothers, sisters, friends, and neighbors. Anything spoken, done, or felt that was contrary to the opinions, *patterns,* or the teachings of Homestead was to be reported to the leadership. We were constantly reminded to "walk in the light." We learned by way of experience. If a leader found out we knew so and so did or said such and such and we hadn't "brought it into the light," we were reproached for not being our "brother's keeper." As parents we were required to police our children and tell the leaders about any behavior the leaders might disapprove of, especially any negative comments about the leaders. Our kids stopped confiding in us. There was no safe place for them to learn from their mistakes. The fear of punishment held us together, not love, and certainly not trust. We were told it was better for family members to expose their own kids' sins rather than have someone outside the family do the exposing. Anything "brought into the light" by someone other than a family member would cast shame upon the parents for not being a good "covering." This gave the leadership an extra layer of reinforcement when it came to keeping us all in check. We all told on each other, which also made their job easier. But there was no safe place to be yourself. I had no real friends.

This *pattern* of tattling undermined the true order of the family. It squelched the possibility of being vulnerable with anyone. To confess my sins to another would be *rewarded* by my confidant spilling my innermost secrets to the leadership. I learned what was acceptable to talk about and what was off limits. I learned safe topics had to do with how wonderful life was at Homestead. Eventually I didn't venture too far from that. Each day I'd scan my mind to remember what I possibly could have said to someone that would have been reported to “those in authority.” My kids who have left Homestead said one of the starkest things they realized about life there was how calculated their lives were. It had become routine to rehearse in their minds how to communicate certain things to avoid their words being misconstrued to mean something that would get them in trouble. I felt the same way.

Throughout my years at Homestead, my heart lurched whenever the phone rang. And if I heard a leader ask, “Could I mention something to you?” I knew I was in trouble once again. Tattling was just gossip disguised as helping someone. I participated in many of those gossip sessions and was the subject of many others. Gossip increases dopamine, the feel-good chemical, and it bonded us together at times. Sadly, those dopamine sessions also caused everyone at Homestead to live in shame. Blair mocked what he called “some sort of Christians” as having love that was about a centimeter deep, yet at Homestead, the relationships were not even that deep.

Patterns

Dress, Hair, and Jewelry

When one of my sons got married, I gave fabric to one of the select seamstresses to make my dress. She stared at the fabric, and then mumbled about how she couldn't use it. She said it wouldn't *hold up*. She chose another fabric and made me a dress I didn't like. I later learned this young seamstress had previously made a dress for a minister's wife for a wedding and had "gotten into trouble" with the clothes police for "not having the wisdom to know the fabric was ungodly." She was scared she'd get in trouble again. I wore a dress I disliked to my son's wedding to keep the seamstress and me out of trouble.

The first time we visited Homestead I wore jeans and makeup. I stuck out among the long dresses and buns and felt a little uncomfortable, so the next time we visited I wore a long dress and left my jewelry behind. Years later when one of my adult sons was a member, he invited an outsider to a Christmas program Homestead was having. She came in a very short dress and sat through the program tugging on it hoping to make it a little longer. She told the lady sitting next to her who happened to have on a long dress that she felt uncomfortable in her short dress. The lady replied, "I made the same mistake last year!" The next year this visitor wore a longer dress.

It didn't take long for anyone interested in Homestead to realize that long dresses and buns were part of the package. I remember wrestling with the idea of giving up all of my trendy Mam'selle clothes and imagining the look of horror on my mother's face when she saw me dressed in a long denim skirt, her hopes of a fashion plate for a daughter dashed.

When visitors asked if we followed certain rules, we were instructed to say, "No one tells us what to do," but if you looked around, all the women looked the same. We knew the rules that governed our lives were called the "patterns of God" that Blair claimed were handed down to him by God. But the truth is that a rule by any other name is still a rule. Little did any visitor know about the mandatory ladies' meetings where Sister Regina, Blair's wife, or her representative reproached us for making worldly clothing choices and instructed us on new patterns. Bobby socks was the topic of one memorable ladies' meeting. I started that trend and was mortified when Sister Regina informed us that bobby socks drew attention to our legs. We could wear either knee socks or no-show socks. I always wanted to be a trendsetter, but being called out for a mistake wasn't the way I had envisioned it. Another time, I wore a loose white sweater to a meeting. Afterwards, Sister Regina called to tell me my outfit was unacceptable and that as an older woman, I was in a place of influence. Again, I was ashamed. When one of my daughters was three years old, I was told she could not wear cap sleeves. The *pattern* was that a child could not wear anything we would not want them to wear as an adult, including pants or rompers for baby girls. It's a miracle our baby girls learned to crawl in long dresses.

Blair ruthlessly pounded into us that our hearts were desperately wicked and we could not trust our carnal minds to know the truth. Instead, we had to humble ourselves to obey his patterns that had "come down from above" and "prove ourselves faithful." To drive the point home, if you violated any of his patterns, you were always asked to "pray about" why you did so. Being asked to pray gave the illusion of humility on the part of the person pointing out your sins, or *ministering* to you as it was called at Homestead.

For example, if you didn't dress like Sister Regina, you would be approached by your minister's wife and asked to "pray about" why you didn't conform to her example. If your clothes were too tight or too short or too bright you would be asked to "pray about" what was in your heart that made you want to draw attention to yourself. If a young girl had plucked her eyebrows, she would be ministered to, and a close eye might be kept on her. One minister, obsessed about being loyal to the leader, carried safety pins in his pocket. He delighted in pulling aside wives and young girls alike and handing them a safety pin because he deemed their blouse too low cut. I saw him as the chief of the clothes police.

When we had a public gathering, like a wedding, the young girls had the opportunity to make special outfits. Those events were times where the leadership had the opportunity to measure how well we were conforming. Whenever our clothes were too tight, too florid, too bright, too short, or too whatever, we got a call from a minister's wife, or our husbands got a call from a minister. If anything became a trend we were all called to a mandatory ladies' meeting. After one wedding where Blair thought the younger generation's clothes were getting too tight, we had a particularly *heavy* ladies' meeting where Sister Regina pointed out in great detail how we weren't *covering* our children sufficiently, meaning watching over them, making sure they followed the patterns.

One Sunday, my daughter wore a rust-colored skirt to a Sunday meeting. After seeing her in the parking lot, Brother Blair had his wife, Regina, call to tell me the color of the skirt was too loud and inappropriate, ending with the phrase, "*That's not us.*" My daughter had worn the same skirt dozens of times over the past two years with no feedback. But to keep within the *patterns*, out went the skirt. Another ladies' meeting focused on a misstep someone made at a bridal shower. A friend had given the bride a pair of pajamas. We spent hours learning how the *pattern* forbidding a woman to wear pants included pajama pants or lounge pants worn when sleeping.

When we first joined, we had a ladies' meeting about hair. Some of the women had mistakenly thought it was ok to trim their hair. Sister Regina explained that we weren't supposed to cut our hair because "long hair" in the Bible meant uncut hair, and our submission to this pattern made us an example to the angels. Strangely though, we were not allowed to say, "We don't cut our hair" to anyone outside of Homestead, even though they taught us that it was biblical. We were to say, "No one tells us what to do!" There are other groups that don't allow women to cut their hair, and when asked about it they answer, "We don't cut our hair." Our vague answers stemmed from Brother Blair not wanting anyone to think Homestead was a cult. It would have been much easier to admit we had rules to follow rather than worrying about giving the right answer to a visitor's question or wearing the wrong thing and getting a dreaded call from a minister that began, "Can I mention something to you?" I put up with all of this because whenever the desire to belong to a group is stronger than the demands, you'll do whatever is required to keep belonging.

The dress patterns even extended to kids when they worked on the farm. Frequently the boys' cowboy hats were deemed too trendy and their sunglasses too worldly. If they wore baseball caps the only logo allowed was the Homestead logo. One day one of my daughters wore a hat with a very large brim while she was harvesting sweet potatoes. There were visitors watching the sweaty kids work in the fields and a minister called to inform me he had sent my daughter home for wearing that hat. I thought she looked cute! Many times my boys were sent home from working on the farm either to change their clothes or stay home and pray about why they wore an "out of it" hat in the first place. Sunglasses became too much for the leaders to deal with most likely because there are so many styles to choose from. So the leaders outlawed them completely. Later on, some of the kids' suffered from permanent eye damage from working outside and not wearing sunglasses.

A few men who grew beards were told to shave them because they weren't spiritual enough to have them. Blair and his sons had beards. I guess the Scripture about imitating your elders didn't apply to beards.

Dietary Patterns

Our son Joe, 25 at the time, and a few of his friends ate breakfast at the restaurant on the land one morning after it was renamed Café Homestead. Joe ordered a cup of coffee. (The word "café" is French for coffee.) After Joe drank his coffee, Curtis received a call from an elder reporting that Joe had ordered a cup of coffee and emphasized that our son had broken the pattern about not drinking coffee. I was exasperated. Café Homestead sells coffee, and my son ordered a cup. He was 25 years old. We wanted to stay in good graces with the leadership, so attempted to agree with the accusation. What else was Curtis to do with that information but say, "Thank you for calling."

When we joined Homestead, tea, coffee, wine, pork, and chocolate were forbidden. Sister Regina authored a book on dietary *patterns* explaining why science backed up abstaining from these things. Brother Blair imposed these dietary restrictions on the congregation by publicly affirming these *patterns* had been given to him by God and as a community, we would be identified by these *patterns*. Just like the Israelites, we would be "set apart."

After we joined, Sister Regina published a dessert cookbook. Fructose was the recommended sweetener in all baking recipes. When a brave and naive member presented the research proving fructose to be horrible for you, they were rebuked for contradicting Sister Regina and not trusting Brother Blair who had "the mind of Christ" and had deemed fructose to be the sugar of choice for all our baking needs. Later when Brother Blair got wind of the negative research on fructose, another sweetener became the dietary sweetener pattern. So the pattern suddenly changed. Blair did not apologize for being wrong before or explain. We received written community announcements each week and one of them had a long attachment about why we could not drink kombucha. It claimed the alcohol content might be too high. The top of the page read, "NO MORE KOMBUCHA!" And yet, by the time we left, lots of people were brewing their own kombucha, so out went another "pattern."

While we dutifully complied with the patterns, we knew the leaders didn't. Children who were assigned the job of cleaning out an elder's RV, found Starbucks cups and chocolate wrappers. (We never understood why the Adamses couldn't let one of their ten children clean up their messes.) The hypocrisy in the leadership who ate chocolate and were seen in the drive-through lane at Starbucks caused a lot of sarcasm and mockery in the young people. We weren't about to say anything about it to anyone in authority. We had come to realize that every time anyone had confronted the leadership, it came back to bite. The accuser always became the accused.

Eventually the book on dietary patterns was thrown out because real scientific research like that about fructose revealed the fallaciousness of all the dietary patterns reported in the book. Tea came to have health benefits. Chocolate helped alleviate depression, although no one at Homestead would ever confess they were depressed for fear of the consequences. We overlooked the insecurity caused by the ever-changing patterns and settled for feeling liberated that we could eat chocolate and drink tea legally. By the time we left, members still weren't allowed to drink coffee, even though it was on the menu at the café.

The *patterns* began to change as the leadership found ways to produce income by adjusting the *patterns*. Shortly after we left

Homestead, they had a coffee shop, a successful tea business, and a successful chocolate business. We read they were hosting cheese and whiskey tastings with a local distillery.

The Homestead website and the sign by the café advertised that the food served at the Café and the grains offered at the gristmill were "locally grown" implying they were produced by Homesteaders on the farm, or on their farms in the area. In truth, early in the morning before the Café opened, semi-trucks lined up outside its back door. The grits and grains sold at the Gristmill were purchased from commercial vendors and the honey was a mixed lot from all over. When my husband mentioned the false advertising, (He feared the consequences if he said that they flat-out lied), he was mocked by the ministers who said he should realize that self-sufficiency was the goal, and it takes time to get there.

We had been there for thirty years.

Entertainment and Vacations

Although they ran the risk of a leader cancelling the trip, vacations were not outright banned. We were allowed to take vacations, but only if the timing and destinations were approved by our minister. Sometimes while we were on vacation, we were called home because Brother Blair had called for a "mandatory community-wide meeting." Other times Blair had fallen sick and might die and we should be there if that were to happen. There were frequent crises like this that we had to maneuver around. If you wanted to take a trip outside of Homestead, the usual *pattern* went like this: The husband called his minister and told him he'd like to take a trip with his family. He'd give the minister the details of the trip such as where they'd like to go and for how long. The minister would reply that he'd pray about it and get back with the husband. Sure enough, the minister would call back, and if he had reservations about the trip, he'd ask the husband to *pray through* about it and get back to him. If the husband still felt like he was supposed to go after he prayed, he'd tell the minister. If the minister still had concerns, he'd ask the husband to pray more. This could go on for a while until the husband told the minister he didn't feel like it was God's will anymore. That's how it worked. A minister would say that if you took a trip that *the brothers* didn't *feel anything about,* then you would be going on the trip *uncovered.* Meaning, if anything bad happened on the trip, it was because you were out of God's will! If you happened to die on an *uncovered* trip you would go to Hell.

The only sport our kids were allowed to play was volleyball because Brother Blair believed competition in all forms was evil and needed to be avoided at all costs. We were to be a community of cooperation. Bike riding for anyone under 18 wasn't allowed because someone almost hit a kid on a bike somewhere on *the Land*. Because of that incident, all the kids had to walk everywhere until they were 16. When they turned 16, they had to go before the bike board and get permission to ride a bike. There were lots of bike laws "on the Land." Blair caught my son, Jonathan, zipping down a steep hill once so we received a call. We had to tell Jonathan he had lost the privilege of riding a bike on *the Land*.

One member bought a kayak so he could take his kids out on a lake nearby. His minister questioned why he would do such a thing and told him to burn it immediately. No other explanation given. (That kayak currently resides behind the ex-member's barn encased in weeds).

Another family went to Colorado on a vacation. The father had decided to take his family snow skiing. He was heavily rebuked for being *carnal* for wanting to ski. Another mother took her son to play tennis at the local tennis center. I was instructed to call her and tell her playing tennis was not allowed. We were allowed to swim in a river or lake if the girls wore a long dress or skirt and the boys wore a shirt and long pants and the girls were not in close proximity with the boys. A young man drowned in a lake. I couldn't help wondering if he drowned because he was required to swim in heavy jeans.

After being members for years, an elder and a wealthy lawyer owned fancy ski boats. Other members in good standing got away with snow skiing and playing tennis. Privileges like that were granted to those who made Blair look good because of their education or wealth or devout loyalty. The majority of the members were held in check by the looming, ever-evolving *patterns* invoked at the whims of leaders who used their power to prove their loyalty to Blair.

Wedding Rings

When we joined Homestead, the pattern for married couples was to wear wedding rings. A few years later a minister from Brazil approached the Homestead leadership about supporting him and the scores of churches he oversaw. Brother Blair's dream was to have churches all over the world under his authority. The minister convinced the Homestead leaders he was legitimate, even to the point that one Homestead leader sent his own daughter and her family to live in Brazil for a while.

The Brazilians had decided Christians shouldn't wear wedding rings. They questioned why we wore wedding rings, so the Homestead leadership took a deep dive into the origin of wedding rings and presented their findings at several mandatory special church meetings. The conclusion was that we were a stumbling block to the Brazilians, so a new *pattern* was introduced. "God said, 'No more wedding rings!'"

Homestead raised money from the Waco congregation for the couples' churches. In my thirty years there, that was the only time I know of that Homestead gave any money to another church or ministry. Soon after the leaders realized they were not coming under Blair's authority. But we didn't go back to wearing wedding rings even after all that. I guess God changed his mind about wedding rings because Brother Blair was willing to change the patterns to have control of hundreds of churches. I put my wedding ring in a drawer and kept on submitting.

By the time we left Homestead, we realized how much time and energy was wasted in a revolving door of ever-changing *patterns* Brother Blair insisted were from God. I came to realize that these *patterns* were used by Blair to meet his own needs of insecurity and lack of worth by dominating and controlling us.

The missing element was love. Blair's motivation wasn't love for the congregation. He mocked unconditional love publicly. His motivation was to protect his own reputation and ideology. Like so many other leaders, he succumbed to the temptation to use power and authority to meet his own needs.

Many years after we joined, Brother Blair wrote a book titled, *Forming Christ's Body* that explained the Scriptures about modesty concerning a woman's spirit, hair, and clothing. It gave a detailed exposé of the dangers concerning the fashion industry. That book was later retitled, *Tolerance*. It should have been named, *Intolerance.* Every explanation we gave anyone about why we lived, dressed, ate, or believed something was based on the evil we were escaping from, whether that was advertising, alcoholism, addiction, promiscuity, divorce, etc. We obviously had no power in ourselves, and the Holy Spirit wasn't strong enough to keep us clean and straight without Blair keeping us in check. Our children were indoctrinated by Blair's god of fear. They gave their lives to his god of fear. They dressed and ate and interacted in apprehension of getting caught. The genuine fear of God morphed into the fear of man. *Fear of man brings a snare. Proverbs 29:25 (KJV)*

Conviction vs. Preference and More Pattern

In our meetings, we repeatedly heard how Brother Blair's leadership kept Homestead on the forefront of God's will on the earth, and how his unique gospel message would eventually reach the entire world. The Scripture, *Do not despise small beginnings, Zechariah 4:10 (NLT)*and songs like, "When You Believe" (with a few revisions) (Stephen Schwartz, 1998) emotionally bolstered these "prophecies."

According to Brother Blair, a prophet was one who affirmed the apostle. In other words, anyone who affirmed Blair. The prophet changed from time to time. A man couldn't be a prophet if he had fallen on Blair's bad side. But whoever was the prophet at any time, his duty was to reaffirm Blair's message during the meeting, usually at the end of it. Those words were to cement the teaching into our brainwashed brains. Blair's success depended on our obedience. To vet our loyalty, we were required to answer multiple questions and sign our names to numerous "conviction" papers every year. If answered correctly, according to the leadership, we were given certain privileges like: becoming a member and taking communion, living on Homestead property, having our homeschooling "covered" by "the church" and having the privilege to home birth using the Homestead midwives. Convictions were the patterns we were willing to die for. A preference would not suffice. Brother Blair had sacrificed for us, so we had the privilege to lay down our lives for his "vision." In one meeting he recounted a dream he implied his wife, Regina, had about people trying to eat with spoons that were so long they couldn't get any food into their mouths. This was a picture of hell because no one in hell would ever think of feeding each other. Vivid images like that were construed to make us think how spiritual Regina was and made the rest of us feel guilty and compelled to sacrifice more. I always thought Regina had dreamed about the long spoons but discovered later that the allegory of the long spoons has been around for centuries and used in many different cultures. Perhaps she did dream of the long spoons. But the sad fact is if anyone in that room had already heard of the allegory, they would not have had the courage to say anything.

According to the dictionary, a conviction is a strongly held belief. A martyr who dies for his faith proves his unswerving devotion to Christ, even unto death. If we were asked whether we were willing to die over our conviction to never cut our hair or wear dresses, we would all have responded with a resounding, "Yes!" But truthfully, we just wanted to be part of the group. The hair and dress and constant second-guessing were part of the package. So we "humbled ourselves" and submitted to the scrutiny of "our convictions."

Homeschooling

According to the "conviction papers," homeschooling was the *general godly pattern* for educating children. At the Thanksgiving Fair, children's writings and crafts were on display in an effort to prove to the community that our "exemplary" education produced well-rounded, above-average kids. The fact was many of my kids' friends could hardly read, much less write a term paper or do more than simple math. For one thing, we were so busy trying to garden, make meals for the sick and moms with new babies, or prepare for tons of fellowships, Friday night meetings, and go to four regular meetings a week, you hardly had time to prepare lesson plans, much less teach them. The busyness kept us in the hamster cage, and the fear of failing the leadership kept us running around in circles. There was little time for thinking and reflecting about what this meant for our children's future. To my own credit, since I lacked confidence in my teaching skills, I made up for some of the lack by reading aloud to my kids every chance I got. All of them became good readers.

No matter how unskilled a teacher you were, homeschooling was the only option. In order to be "covered" by "the church" you had to answer about sixty questions testing your conviction. (There was no test of your ability to teach.) To be a member in good standing, our answers had to please our ministers. If our answers passed muster, the leadership agreed to stand by us if we were taken to court. If we failed in some way, we would be "uncovered" or basically abandoned by those who pledged at communion to stand by us. Our "covering" would be revoked. If taken to court for some reason, we'd be on our own. Rather than the community coming around the family to offer support, the family would be denied help from "the body" because they had not earned it. Then, the family would be humiliated, criticized, and sidelined because they didn't live up to the perfect standard they agreed upon when they completed the homeschool conviction papers. If your answers were inadequate or you missed the mark in your homeschooling, you were told to *pray through* to understand why there wasn't "full conviction" on your part. Some families were put on *Friday night status* until they came to a "complete conviction." This meant they were not allowed to go to Sunday church meetings and had to be given permission to attend a church function. If you were not allowed to attend Sunday church meetings, you were denied communion, (which was only twice each year). You had to prove yourself by working your way back to the privilege of attending church.

Living on the Land

If anyone wanted to live on "the Land," meaning the church-owned farm, the leaders required them to fill out a *conviction paper* called "Land Settlement Agreement." These papers included a requirement for everyone who lived in a mobile home (most everyone) to build a site-built house as soon as possible. The worst of the mobile homes, like the ones that had been previously flooded, were tucked in the woods out of sight. If someone lived in a mobile home, they at least owned their home. Homestead owned the land that the houses and mobile homes were on. We built a house on the land (that we bought for them,) and we paid rent for many years. We convinced ourselves this was God's will.

The Water Situation

There had never been a master plan to install a decent water system on the Homestead land. Pipes were laid here and there and never marked, so digging a hole for a fencepost or anything else risked hitting a water line, leaving the entire community without water. Then, a plumber had to be tracked down to remedy the situation as we watched a geyser in the yard.

The plumbing system at our house was a giant PVC puzzle. With each new installation, we put in a new filtration system, more pipes, and seemingly miles of intake and exit water lines, which zigzagged along the walls of the shop behind our house. The well water was full of iron, and lots of other minerals. Without a filter it came out of the faucet red. We frequently replaced toilets and appliances due to the hard water clogging them up. We made multiple efforts to change the hard calcium, red iron water from the Homestead well into clear, usable water. There also were pipes and water lines around the perimeter of the shop that ran everywhere and nowhere all at the same time. Most of them went to some abandoned device that had never been removed.

At times, in order to wipe out any invading bacteria, gallons of bleach were dumped in the big, black, algae-invading cisterns. One visitor who stayed at the Homestead guest house said she took a shower and came out a bleached blonde.

This was the same scenario for all the water systems on Brazos de Dios, the name given to the Homestead land except one. Brother Blair's family had an expensive water filtration system with a water softener at his house. The community-salaried farm manager maintained the Adams' water system on an almost daily basis. He regularly called one of our sons to haul 50-pound bags of salt up the hill behind the house to feed the water softener. For the rest of us the water at Homestead was a source of misery not only because of all the iron and the awful smell, but also because we so often didn't have any. When my water was cut off, I'd call a neighbor to see if their water was off or if something was wrong with one of our many filtration systems. Many of the people who installed the plumbing were novices assigned to that work on that particular day. A lot of the underground lines had been buried by young boys on a hot workday, and they weren't trenched deep enough.

Putting up with this ridiculous water situation was part of our *sacrifice* of being in the "center of God's will." We could have had perfectly clean and clear water like Brother Blair and all of his children's families had, but Brother Blair's goal of self-sufficiency was rooted in his hatred for the government and his own desire to control others. He consistently claimed that he didn't want to be dependent on a public water company, so the rest of us got used to the water cutting off. We adjusted to wearing orange clothes.

By God's grace, no one had gotten sick, though there were quite a few kidney stones because of the high levels of calcium in the water. Because Blair believed he was God, the leadership thought they could live above the law, at least until a crisis woke them up.

Order of the Household

When a couple married, the husband was to be the "covering" for his wife and the head of his family. The husband was assigned a minister to be "over him." This seemed to work organically as the congregation was divided into small groups that met on Friday nights. We were all assigned to a small group. Visitors were invited to these Friday night meetings, but Sunday meetings were closed to all "outsiders." For all the perfection the group portrays to the outside world, it's hardly immune from sin. The common sins among the "outside" population in general have been rife at Homestead, contrary to the wholesome image they wish to show to the outside world. We mostly found out someone had gotten into trouble when he or she "humbled themselves" and repented before the congregation. The one apologizing had to validate that "the brothers" were right and conclude by repledging their loyalty to the leadership. When members no longer came to Sunday meetings, we knew they were "in trouble" and were "working their way" back into "good standing." The same was true if someone was not at a communion service.

Trying to live up to this image of perfection caused me to live in fear of failing the leadership and suffering the consequences of being "disfellowshipped." A husband could displease the leadership by dishonoring them (questioning their authority). If so, he was said to have failed in his role as a "covering" for his family. The "covering" over the family was then transferred to the wife's minister, who would assume the role of "covering" the family. This now displaced husband lost his "place of authority" in his family, humiliating him more. The wife was then instructed to tattle on her husband to her minister which seriously strained the relationship between the wife and husband. Not only did this demoralize the man, but it also stripped him of respect from his children.

If parents failed in meeting the *patterns* of raising their children or their children were rebellious, they ran the risk of having their children removed from the home and raised by *more qualified* adults picked by the leadership. In the hope of reforming a rebellious teenage girl, this often meant she would be assigned to work in a leader's home or for a family the leaders felt was qualified. She would babysit, clean, and cook for the family. The leaders benefitted by receiving free labor while the young girl would in return learn submission and hopefully be able to one day be trusted by the leadership. Perhaps she might one day be good enough to get married. The girl's own mother was punished for her failure as a "covering" and had to adjust to not having her own daughter's help in her home. When I look back on this practice, I realize how pervasive it was. Over and over, fragile families simply fell apart, and others limped along until the father (or mother) caved in and "got back into submission." Brother Blair and his family were exempt from this sort of "discipline." He implemented a loophole when it came to his own sins or the sins of his kids. (which were plenty). We were instructed when certain crises happened concerning him or his children that we were to cover his sins just as Noah's sons covered him with a robe when he was drunk and naked in his tent. In these cases we were to "cover" their sins by overlooking them and not telling anybody.

In other words, our leader was allowed to fail, but we weren't.

The role of women

The role of women was to have children, cook, keep house, teach their children, serve their husbands, and have more children. The husband job was to keep the women in check. Brother Blair frequently used the comparison of mythology and Scripture. One elder taught the "order of the household" at a public event. *Pater*, he said (Latin for fatherhood) came down from above. Patriarchy was ordained of God and came down from heaven. The origin of the word *mater,* the root of "matriarchy" (motherhood) came from material from below. The women were to be ruled over from above. Women were usually the guilty party because Eve ate the apple first. This isn't anything new when it comes to patriarchal cultures. Women are made to serve the men, and those lines are clearly defined. Visiting women with vibrant personalities were often the subject of much discussion among the ministers. One friend of mine who visited for eight years was never allowed to join because the leadership feared she could not be controlled. She and her husband were finally told they were not welcome at any Homestead function. One entrepreneurial woman started a prosperous business out of her home. The ministers felt threatened by her success so they "heavily ministered" to her husband for letting her get out of control and accused him of being a wimp of a man. In the end her business became so profitable the leaders were happy to get their tithe from it.

Midwifery and Home Birth

We were taught that homebirth, was a "general godly pattern," meaning that God's perfect will was for all births to take place at home. If we wanted to have our babies with the Homestead midwives and be "covered" by the "church," we had to fill out the *Homebirth Conviction* papers. These questions were to test our conviction to homebirth. After

I had answered these sixty questions a few times, I realized they all asked the same question from different angles: If something went wrong in the birth, who was responsible? If everything went by the book the midwives would be there to help me but if something went wrong, then the parents would take the blame and basically be on their own. Since the Homestead midwives were not licensed, the mom was to be transported to the hospital with no support from these people who were supposed to be her friends. She was to tell the doctor that she had had no prenatal care and that she planned on having her husband deliver her baby.

The fact was, the midwives provided pre- to postnatal care and kept detailed records of everything, but when things went awry, they stepped out of the picture. I didn't see it at the time, but later realized they didn't want to get in trouble with the law and tarnish their reputation among the medical community. The leaders claimed the reason the midwives weren't licensed was because midwifery was a "ministry" of the church. Since Blair's goal was protecting Homestead's reputation, those moms who ended up being transported to a hospital were often instructed to lie to the doctors at the hospital. It sounded nice to help your sisters in Christ in birth but how much to tell an outsider was a bit hazy. I never had to be transported to the hospital, but many others did, and some were first time moms who felt abandoned by those who they had trusted to help them. Since we lived in fear of displeasing those in authority, members were willing to lie in public to "cover" them and humiliate themselves by being perceived by the doctor as naive nincompoops. The women at Homestead can be spotted a mile away, so, of course, the doctors recognized immediately they were part of the group. But those were the conditions we signed our names to.

Unfortunately for some, the midwives didn't possess the skill or legal license to repair a more complicated tear resulting from a birth, and not wanting the community to come under scrutiny among the medical community, left some young moms to live with pain and deformity the rest of their lives. But because it had been drilled into the mom not to question, she silently lived with the terrible consequences. Some were so naive that they accepted the pain and suffering as normal. I knew of a mom who needlessly suffered excruciating pain because her midwife claimed she was fearful and lacked faith. The midwife refused to consider there might be a complication with the birth. When the mother was finally transported to the hospital, the doctor informed her that she had an ectopic pregnancy. Some of these cases went undiagnosed for so long it's a miracle the mother didn't die. All these cases were completely avoidable. The arrogance of the unlicensed midwives led to a lack of care for the pregnant moms. In these cases a midwife's "feelings" led to denying the mom proper medical treatment. A lack of love was at the root of the botched jobs.

For many years after we joined, if someone had a miscarriage, a "spiritual" investigation immediately ensued because a miscarriage meant there must be sin in the parents. The poor, weak, disappointed, and grieving parents were subjected to ongoing questions and told to "pray through" to see what caused the misfortune. There was literally no rest for the weary. That scenario played out whenever Brother Blair or his wife Regina was afflicted by sickness or some sort of malady. I recall Sister Regina's sickness signaled "sin in the camp," and a witch hunt would begin to find the culprit. When she had a miscarriage, there was no witch hunt.

When my father was diagnosed with dementia, Brother Howard told me all autoimmune diseases were *spiritual*, meaning that those diseases were caused by the afflicted person's sin. A few years later when Regina and several of the Adams' children were diagnosed with autoimmune diseases, I reminded Howard of what he had emphatically told me. He immediately responded, "The Adamses are not culpable. They are under a spiritual attack." They assumed one or more members had sinned, thereby bringing disaster on Blair, his family, and his reputation by our actions.

I recognize everyone's actions have consequences, but this inherent belief taught by the leadership kept everyone living in fear, trying to make sure they weren't the cause of an affliction on our leader or a member of his family. Midwifery and home birth highlighted this doctrine on many levels. For the midwives as well as the moms and dads, good outcomes depended on our vigilance to the perfection we pursued. One slip up spelled doom.

One common reason for slip ups, the leaders drilled into us, was a lack of faith. Faith at Homestead meant faith in the leadership and our willingness to submit to them. Most of the midwives had experience, but limited training. They weren't licensed to practice as midwives, so they didn't think they had to obey state law. That made it convenient for the midwives to make decisions contrary to the requirements a licensed midwife would be bound by. If a birth went well, everyone was happy, but sometimes a midwife made decisions based on what she felt in her heart about the mom or situation rather than what the law required. And sometimes that had bad consequences.

I attended a birth where a mom labored unsuccessfully for two days. One of the attending midwives mentioned transporting the mom to the hospital. Being a fearful person by nature, her fear was perceived by another of the midwives (by this point four midwives were on the scene) as a "lack of faith." All attention then zeroed in on that midwife's lack of faith, rather than the birth at hand.

The mother eventually was transferred to the hospital where she had a C-section. The fearful midwife endured "ministry" by the leading midwife in the form of being shamed for her lack of faith and blamed for the mother's lack of faith that landed her in the hospital. The guilty midwife was removed from the midwifery "ministry" for many years. Both she and the mother repented publicly before a thousand people for their lack of faith, ending the testimony with a renewed commitment to the leadership.

I know of a stillbirth where the baby was denied the dignity of being named, or any recognition of being born, and the leaders would not allow the parents to file a birth or death certificate as required by law, yet the baby's body occupies a grave in the Homestead cemetery. I believe that was to prevent drawing attention to the midwifery practices in an effort to keep up what they erroneously perceived as their sterling reputation. At those times, the feelings of the parents didn't really matter. That was their way of upholding their covenant.

A young first-time mom stood in my kitchen at a fellowship and mentioned that she thought she should have a C-section. Somehow her midwife found out the mom was worried about her birth. The midwife perceived the pregnant girl as dramatic and fear-based. The midwife immediately began to "minister" to her about her lack of faith. This "ministry" usually entailed shaming the person for being fearful and threatening to punish her by taking away the privilege of having her baby with her sisters, the midwives. She'd have to find someone "outside" to deliver her baby and she was due fairly soon.

The young mom, now feeling shame and fear, had to dig down deep in her heart to find the sin that was causing her to doubt her midwives and her covenant. She repented repeatedly of her lack of trust publicly in small group meetings and church-wide meetings and renewed her pledge to trust the leadership. She had proved herself to the "body," who had no idea what her issue was but understood she had blown it somehow.

After enduring an arduous birth, her baby was born with a fairly common complication that would have compelled a licensed midwife by law to transport the baby to the hospital. Instead, the midwife transported the baby to Homestead's medical clinic and tried to use equipment that she had no training or license to use. The doctor trained to use it was in another state at the time and tried to assist the midwife over the phone, but to no avail. She finally transported the baby to the hospital where the baby was put on life support and declared dead a few days later.

Perhaps this baby would have died anyway. We'll never know. But I witnessed the conflict and desperation in this midwife. She knew she might have caused the baby's death because she refused to listen to the mother's concerns in the first place. Now she lives with that for the rest of her life.

Jesus understands our fears and struggle to trust, but this midwife unfortunately stood in God's place and shamed this young mom into declaring faith, when in reality she just wanted to stay in good standing. I believe the mom's testimony came from a place of shame and fear, not faith in God. To deflect the truth about the birth and draw any negative attention away from midwifery practices, the leadership staged an enormous funeral for this baby and invited all the attending outside medical staff. A meal followed at the reception. Soon after, the young dad was given a ministerial position. I wonder if this was to divert attention from blaming the midwife for possibly killing their baby.

Divide and Conquer and How it all Plays Out (One Example of Many)

A couple with seven children rented a small house on the Homestead property that they soon outgrew. The mom was having a hard time homeschooling her children while being expected to attend Tuesday night prayer meetings, Wednesday night meetings, Friday night group meetings, Saturday workdays, and Sunday meetings. Then there were the continuous birthday and anniversary fellowships, showers, weddings, funerals, and important special meetings that our lives revolved around.

She was also expected to prepare meals for those who needed support. If she admitted she wasn't able to volunteer to make a meal or help someone else in any way, she would receive a call from the minister's wife, interrogating her as to why she didn't have the faith to be stretched and serve *the body*. The mom, afraid to confess that she didn't feel adequate for the task and her children were not doing well in school, succumbed to the pressure given by the minister's wife, saying she would *pray through* the situation. Feeling like a failure as a mother, wife, and teacher, she found the faith to stretch and prepare a meal for her friend.

Since she was on a tight budget, she prepared the best meal she could with the limited resources she had. Because the meal was heavy on carbs, she received another call from the minister's wife, informing her that the meal didn't hit the mark. She was admonished because her friend just gave birth and needed more proteins and greens so her body could produce nourishing milk for her baby. Knocked down another notch, the mother of seven was at her breaking point.

The mother, ill-equipped to educate her ever-growing family, began to crack under the scrutiny of her homeschool advisor and minister's wife. The father, raised by a single mother, had a poor education, married young, and immediately started a family without financial savings. He had construction skills, but he was deemed to be financially irresponsible for his family. The ministers concluded this family had lost the privilege of living on "the Land" and were told to move off "the Land."

By now the mom was expecting another baby and trying to pack up her house, teach her children, and serve the community that she had failed by her lack of faith. They rented a mobile home near the Homestead property where they hoped to have a new start and work their way back into the leaderships'good graces. She was not deemed worthy to have her baby with the midwives, so they had to make other arrangements for their upcoming birth.

Year-end evaluations snuck up before the Thanksgiving Fair, and the children performed poorly, especially in Greek. Greek had only been introduced as a required course in the last few years, and the mom really didn't understand how to teach it. In fact, not many of us did. If children could memorize the vocabulary just enough to pass the test, did they really know Greek?

Because the mom did a poor job teaching Greek, and because her children performed poorly on the test, along with having to move off "the Land," the parents were not allowed to take communion. They were told they might bring a reproach on Homestead by outsiders who found out they had inadequately educated their children, which might hurt Homestead's sterling reputation.

Ashamed, the family felt isolated, and the father considered leaving Homestead. He confessed his thoughts to his minister, and immediately the wife was given permission to return to Friday night meetings. The older children sat in meetings that described the terrible fate of covenant breakers, and they began to view their father as a second-rate citizen. After all, they were taught he was a Judas, a betrayer, for considering breaking his vow to Homestead. The older children gave in to the pressure to prove their father wrong and pledged their lives to the leadership of Homestead. The father saw what the leadership was doing to his family, so he left Homestead.

At meetings, members were convinced these children needed their support, so they surrounded the oldest child and prayed for him, which meant they yelled in his ears, "Be faithful to God and God will bring your dad around. You can win him back!"

The oldest child was told that he had a call on his life – he would help save his pitiful, backslidden dad. But instead of loving his dad, he considered himself better than his dad, refusing to listen or take counsel from him. After all, his dad had become a pagan dad and unworthy of a son's attention. This insubordination ran rampant through the family and the dad became an outcast in his own home. All the teaching about honoring parents and showing respect vanished when the ministers blamed and shamed the dad. That teaching only applied to parents who were loyal to Blair and his leadership. And so, the ministers won. They divided and conquered yet another family at Homestead.

Because the dad no longer wanted to be part of Homestead, he lost his place in what Brother Blair called the *order*, and the dad's former minister took his place in the family. The wife's loyalty was divided between her minister and her husband. She privately talked to her minister about her husband and was instructed to not talk with her husband about the conversation. The children were subtly encouraged to disregard and disrespect their dad, and their egos grew by leaps and bounds. They grew into little Pharisees who lorded it over their father, loving the leaders' attention. They were earning their place in the *kingdom*, all the while destroying their family.

Meanwhile, the dad who needed love and relationships, attended a church in town, and to the amazement of people at Homestead, became financially successful, more responsible, and happy. No one could deny the positive changes. But the Homestead ministers hated the source of those changes. They couldn't view the people in the church he was attending as real Christians! How could he be changing?

Because of this father's determination, he continued to live with his wife and children although he was not allowed to participate in any Homestead activities including his own child's birthday party. This one messed-up family would be one too many, but there are many disillusioned people, failed marriages, and ruined lives in the wake of Brother Blair's "ministry."

Jonathan and Clinging to the Vine

Jonathan, my child number two and second boy, arrived three weeks early after a 48-hour labor. I lay in the hospital bed waiting for the nurse to swing open the door and wheel in the clear plastic tub containing my newborn miracle. All night I waited and the next morning I was practically running down the hall looking for him. The nurse at her post pointed to the pediatrician who happened to be bent over my baby at that moment. I desperately looked through the glass that divided the world from the newborns and saw a huge red heart shaped device on Jonathan's chest. "What's wrong with him?" I yelled through the glass trying to get the doctor's attention. He disconnected the monitor and walked into the viewing area with a big smile on his face.

"We had to keep an eye on him overnight," he said. I thought maybe he should hook me up to the heart-shaped monitor, my heart was beating so fast. He finally realized I was upset and casually said, "His heart beats very slowly. He has a very strong heart though. I imagine he'll be a long-distance runner." He walked off and instructed the nurse to let me have my baby.

Of all nine of my kids, Jonathan ranks at the top as one of the easiest babies. He was easily consolable, happy and went to sleep with little fuss. While the doctor was right about the long-distance runner, he totally missed that he would be a sprinter, too. Jonathan played long and hard and was the source of a lot of our entertainment. At only 10 months old, Jonathan, who had recently learned to walk, climbed up the wooden jungle gym attached to our swing set and hung from the top rung until his little ten-month-old arms grew tired before he dropped into my arms. Not to be deterred, he climbed back up to the top rung and fell off again. To Jonathan, bumps and bruises meant he had had a good day.

When we went swimming, he'd walk straight into the pool. I'd gasp as I saw those big blue eyes looking up in wonder, and I'd jump in and fish him out. If I wasn't careful, he'd jump right back in. He never went through the phase of being afraid of water like the rest of my kids did when they were learning to swim. He was a born fish.

When Jonathan was two, my first daughter, who was eight weeks old, was in her crib for a nap. A little while later, to my horror, I saw Jonathan holding his little sister by the neck and dragging her down the hallway towards my room. Before I could ask him what on earth he was doing, he innocently looked up at me and said, "She was crying." Somehow, he had pulled her up and over the side of the crib. No wonder she was crying!

Jonathan didn't start out walking; he ran with all the strength of his slow beating heart. The older he grew, the rougher he got with his siblings. He'd wrestle them on land and dunk them when they were in the water. He'd inflict bruises and welts and felt justified in winning the skirmish. While some of my children lied or tried to manipulate me, the one thing I can say about Jonathan is he was honest. If he hit his brother and I questioned him about it, he'd say, "I was mad at him!" At least we knew where he stood. I was too busy chasing him around to ponder for long how his gifts and talents might mold his life's purpose. I just wanted everyone to survive.

Many times, I thought I should take Jonathan to be evaluated by a professional for his hyperactivity and dyslexia, but no one did that in the Fellowship. Doctors and professionals in general were scorned by its leaders for being "specialists." Brother Blair disdained any licensing or government control, so I silently complied and resorted to spanking excessively and yelling in frustration so our family could measure up to the leader's expectations.

We drove back and forth from Dallas to Austin for the first few years of going to Fellowship meetings, and it seemed every time Jonathan was around other kids, we had something to deal with. The more I disciplined him, the harder he fought me and the more exhausted I became. I talked frequently about honor to my young children trying to impart on their level the teaching we were receiving. I would correct what they said by saying, "That doesn't honor the Lord." The kids endured long prayer times where I'd read to them from "Building Christian Character," a book Brother Blair wrote contrasting good and bad character using examples in the Bible. Brother Howard called Curtis repeatedly about Jonathan wrestling with other kids or playing with pretend guns. We must have said, "Keep your hands to yourself," a million times. To no avail. He couldn't do it.

After one weekend in Austin, Brother Howard called Curtis and said Jonathan had brought GI Joe toys to play with at his house. He let us know we had joined a nonviolent community and those toys were unacceptable. GI Joe men did not fit within the "patterns." We were exposing other kids to the military, and we needed to see how that dishonored Brother Blair's "patterns" that included not voting, not serving on a jury, and not serving in the military. We got rid of those toys. Howard made sure we understood that was a serious offense. I was getting the point that we had to nip these things in the bud before we raised criminals or soldiers. I was embarrassed he had to call and felt like a bad parent for allowing my son to play with such violent toys. I had so much to learn. With each phone call came the opportunity to help Jonathan conform to the high standard we had committed to. I did the only thing that seemed right to me at the time and came down hard on Jonathan each time he disobeyed. Howard said we needed to break his will, so that is what I intended to do.

We bought the wrong kind of jeans at times. Brother Howard would tell us they were too trendy. They didn't fit within the clothes "pattern." We thought they were just plain old Wranglers. Once when Jonathan was a young teenager, we received a call claiming he was trying to be cool like the Marlborough Man by wearing a certain cowboy hat and trendy sunglasses.

I'd sigh and wonder if I was the worst mom in the Fellowship. When we finally moved to the Homestead farm, the calls about Jonathan's behavior multiplied and the accusations became more serious. If a group of boys had been working on the farm and said something *dishonoring* about a "brother," especially an elder, we'd get a call and have to interrogate Jonathan about exactly what he said and to whom. Sometimes calls flew back and forth from one parent to a minister to another parent and so forth-- until no one remembered what the initial transgression was. Those calls took priority over school because dishonor was the biggest offense. Dishonor at Homestead after all was the root of all sin. It could lead people right out of the Fellowship which meant they'd lose out with God.

My efforts at disciplining Jonathan yielded little improvement. The ministers labeled him a troublemaker and eventually he couldn't do anything right. If any "sin" came into the light, meaning that something bad had happened that no one confessed to, Jonathan was the first suspect. The older he got the more tension mounted in my life as I tried to keep a lid on his life and expose him to as few people as possible. We wanted him to take all the craft classes and have the privilege of working on the farm, but because he was known as a troublemaker no one wanted him in their classes. That included the teachers as well as the parents. The leaders made clear that the consequence of sin was losing the privilege of being in fellowship with others. If a child didn't "honor the order," meaning the leaders, he would be disfellowshipped and not allowed to be with other kids. So Jonathan stayed at home like a lion in the enclosure at the zoo. Full of energy and allowed to go nowhere. To get out some energy, on a few occasions Jonathan put two of his younger siblings in our big Radio Flyer wagon and pushed them to the edge of the high bluff we lived on. He'd grab the racing wagon just before they flew off the edge and crashed to their deaths! We learned the meaning of being disfellowshipped because that's what Jonathan was most of the time he lived with us. He was alone in his room. Frustrated.

As Jonathan grew to be an older teenager, we worried about his fate in the Fellowship. We knew the "pattern" was if a kid turned 18 and wasn't inclined to be baptized, he had to move away from his family. We had witnessed many kids leave home unprepared for life outside the Fellowship. The leadership embedded in the members that this was the Lord's will. The leaders' hope was the kid would hit rock bottom and return home repentant and begging to join. Jonathan grew more restless and miserable with each passing lonely day. At the multitude of required meetings we attended he connected, undetected, with two of Brother Blair's kids. We were supposed to be "covering" our children at all meetings. That meant we were to listen to every word they said to anyone else. That was the "pattern," but it made it hard to visit with anyone and would have saved a lot of trouble if I had just gone home as soon as we were dismissed. Two of the Adams kids scared me. That would have been the end of my relationship with the Adamses if Brother Blair knew I thought that. That would be terribly dishonoring. Brother Blair's kids were untouchable. They had some bad kids, but having "Adams" as their last name guaranteed impunity. The last name Brown guaranteed an investigation and usually guilty until proven innocent. By that time, we were too tired to care.

I gave up on trying to make Jonathan conform. I was so busy with his siblings I slowly lost connection with him. I feared he'd leave us and the Fellowship as so many other kids had, so I didn't want to push him too much. There were few intact families in the Fellowship once the kids grew up. When our kids were little, I never imagined they'd ever want to leave us. I thought we'd live happily ever after. It was just that Jonathan was having a harder time than the rest of them. So when he created an exercise course in the woods by our house and started a disciplined training program, I did nothing about it.

Brother Blair never called us directly, and I imagine that was true for everyone else. He communicated his displeasure with Curtis through Brother Howard until Blair kicked Howard's family off "the Land." Then Tzafrir became the main enforcer. Sometimes Regina, his wife, called me if Blair was burdened by something we or our kids had done. Then when Aber turned twenty, Blair had him call us sometimes. It was dishonoring to burden Brother Blair. He had so many weighty matters to deal with. That's why we needed to keep Jonathan in line, so Brother Blair would not be distracted from the work God had called him to do. He communicated through Brother Howard that Jonathan had been a bad influence on two of his sons, and he had the muscles to prove it. Apparently, Jonathan was lifting weights with Brother Blair's sons, and that wasn't within the "patterns." "That was carnal," said Brother Howard.

Brother Blair blamed Jonathan for his boys' interest in the military, even though Isaac was older than Jonathan. Blair claimed it was our fault for not "staying on top of our son." The ministers told us our kids had been meeting in the field below our house by the river smoking cigarettes, drinking beer, looking at pornography and working out. Since Jonathan didn't have his license yet, we assumed the contraband came from the Adams boys, which was confirmed by Jonathan when we asked him. Isaac Adams was several years older than Jonathan and owned a vehicle so we figured it came from him. But Brother Blair was convinced it all came from Jonathan and everything was his fault. Our good relationship with Brother Blair and his wife cooled. Curtis and I began to feel the isolation Jonathan felt. We felt like we were being punished for being bad parents and corrupting Blair's kids. I tried to keep Jonathan far from Brother Blair's kids, but they found ways to sneak off together. One night I left a prayer meeting early. Jonathan had stayed home sick but when I walked into our house I heard someone scurrying around. I found Brother Blair's son, Isaac, trying to hide in Jonathan's room. We knew Brother Blair would blame Jonathan for his son being in our house. Not long after that, the Adams boys joined the military. After short stints, they both returned home, only to leave and return to the Fellowship repeatedly.

One day, when Jonathan was 17, he was nowhere to be found. My heart broke when it got late, and he never came home. I paced around the house hoping he'd walk in any minute. I walked into his room where all his stuff still was and wondered if he'd come back to get it. I felt like he had died and a part of me with him. I knew other kids who reached Jonathan's age had made a choice between their family and "the world." Now, Jonathan had made that choice. That's what honor at Homestead required. Always a choice between God and "the world." He wouldn't be allowed to come back "on the Land." We would have to reject him and vilify him because he was going to hell, and we would want our other kids to know that was their fate if they left too. He'd be used as an example from the pulpit as a traitor just as others who left had been.

He had bought a small truck in preparation for leaving us. My worst nightmare had come true. Jonathan had no life or future at Homestead. He grew tired of being alone and ostracized by the leadership. He didn't fit in, and the leaders wanted him to leave because he might influence other young people. I had joined this group believing my children would grow up in a safe, wholesome environment and want to be with us forever. I imagined our grandkids would live near us. Never did I think they'd be exposed by the leaders' children to every vice imaginable. (Things far worse than those I mentioned above.)

Jonathan, like all kids approaching their eighteenth birthday, was given an ultimatum to join Homestead and be baptized or leave home. Jonathan felt the pressure knowing that if he left, he would lose contact with us. Pressure came in the form of what we called *heavy meetings* where groups of people surrounded a young person and yelled close to their ear, "Repent! Don't throw away your miracle!" Some spoke in tongues in hopes the recipient would "catch the spirit" and break out in "tongues" themselves!

Frequently a song like Whitney Houston's, "When You Believe" was sung to commemorate the victory along with a run around the building. If the person failed to respond, we could expect a somber and abrupt ending to the meeting. The clear message conveyed was the inevitable demise of the person who decided to leave. They encouraged us to pray for bad things to happen to the wayward person, in hopes they would return. Over the years, some who hit rock bottom came back out of desperation.

By the time he left home, Jonathan's mind was made up to become a Marine. I cried and grieved over losing him, yet I believed the church leadership, that in flinging him into the world unprepared, we were doing the right thing.

Brother Howard said we needed to cling to the vine (the leadership) even tighter. Some friends knew our grief because they too had "lost" one or more of their children to "the world." They had a wedding anniversary party for us where we sang songs about being a family, like "We're part of a family that's been born again...," knowing we'd committed to these people, our true family. Because, like the song we learned when we first joined, "We left our kinfolk gladly..." We did what they said and swallowed our grief and clung ever tighter to the vine.

Like so many others, I listened to the lies the leaders spoke about Jonathan and never stood up for him. I justified cruel treatment to the very one God gave me to nurture. One time, Jonathan drove 24 hours from Camp Pendleton in California to visit us. We refused to let him come to our house because we were afraid of what the leaders would think. We lived in fear of people who controlled us, people who didn't love Jonathan. Still, we treated him like scum, all in the name of God, yet he refused to stop loving us.

The disciplined training he had undertaken in the woods outside our house helped him through bootcamp and through a harrowing deployment in Iraq where he witnessed many of his friends' deaths. I can't help but relate his pulling his sister out of her crib and down the hall to the many occasions he's pulled a wounded or dead Marine away from conflict. Such as the time his Humvee was blown up by a mine in Iraq. The times he walked into the swimming pool prepared Jonathan to hold a record for staying underwater the longest while training with a 90-pound pack on his back. He literally died twice, but was determined to pass the test. And as for the jungle gym, he has climbed up and down dangerous terrain and in and out of caves in Afghanistan, Iraq and the Philippines. Although he tried to please us and fit into the Fellowship mold, it simply wasn't his calling. It was either Homestead or "the world." And he did the right thing and chose "the world."

Part Three

A Little Background

Homestead had levels of membership. Everyone started out as a visitor, but when someone's intentions became more serious, they were groomed to become a member. First stop on that course, you would be asked to read books the founder wrote. Then you were quizzed on them, asked to answer lists of questions in writing that the ministers would evaluate. From your answers, they would decide if you were ready to make a "covenant" with them. If you questioned the leaders' actions in the future, they might reference your answers, reminding you that you had covenanted with them that you would trust them and not question their authority.

The next step was usually baptism. If you had already been baptized *in Jesus' name only,* then you simply declared your intention to be bound to Homestead and the leadership for life. If you had been baptized in the name of the Father and of the Son and of the Holy Spirit you needed to be rebaptized into Homestead and declare your intention to be bound to Homestead and its leadership. The leaders made it clear by mocking every denomination including Baptists, Methodists, Presbyterians, Lutherans, Catholics, etc...that Trinitarians were not saved, and the only way to heaven was to be baptized in Jesus' name only. That was what they taught was the only correct way to be baptized.

Upon coming out of the water you were declared a *situational member* and started out your service to the community with a clean slate or *in good standing* as they called it. The more you pleased the leadership, you might become someone considered loyal and trustworthy which would earn you *transitional status*. This status meant you had submitted to the leaders even if you disagreed with them, followed the "patterns," and sacrificed your time by serving the community. When members committed *biblical sins* such as adultery, lying, or stealing, the leaders claimed these were sins that *gave God a black eye*, because they tarnished Homestead's sterling reputation in the public's eye. After the guilty came to repentance for harming the community's reputation, they stood to confess their repentance to the congregation. Conversely, *Homestead sin* that was brought before the congregation had to do with questioning *authority* and therefore not having faith in the leaders. Since as a member they had signed a covenant to be loyal to the leadership, they were guilty of breaking their covenant simply by questioning. Any member who committed either a biblical or *Homestead sin* might be *disassociated*, meaning they were demoted and could not attend Sunday meetings unless given permission. In those *heavy* meetings, as we called them, the leaders intentionally tried to put fear in the rest of us. We didn't want to go through that humiliation publicly, so we secretly vowed to not fail like that person did. Person after person, week after week, confessed their "sin" of mistrust of the leadership and recommitted their lives to Blair and the others he appointed.

As I've mentioned before, when a member was *disassociated*, they could not take communion. They were also put on *Friday night status*, meaning they could not attend Sunday meetings or certain community events. Only the members in good standing were welcome at those.

Members who were *disassociated* also had to be invited to any community activities and were heavily monitored by their minister. In other words, disassociation sent the member to the bottom rung of the ladder of membership. If they had a spouse or family they didn't want to be separated from, they had to start climbing up all over again. Some gave up the fight and left.

If someone left Homestead or was kicked out, he or she was what we called *disfellowshipped*. No matter the reason someone left or was made to leave, they were labeled *bitter*. Leaving Homestead was considered a sin because it meant you broke your covenant with the leadership. Rejecting the covenant with the leadership meant rejecting God which meant that you were on your way to Hell. It didn't matter what precipitated your leaving, even if someone in leadership sinned against you. Because the leadership professed to have the literal "mind of Christ," it was impossible for them to be wrong.

Brother Blair instructed his appointed leaders to never *apologize down*. Members were to apologize to the leaders for their every sin, but leaders were never to apologize for any bad behavior on their part to a member. Consequently, issues between members and leaders were never resolved.

Any time someone left Homestead and spoke about their experience there, or Homestead received bad publicity whether by print, broadcast or digital media, the leadership claimed Satan was attacking the church and Brother Blair was being persecuted because of his sacrifice to the Lord. The leaders claimed that there was sin *in the camp* and this sin had left *a hole in the wall of protection around Homestead*. This left *the church* precariously vulnerable to the *enemy*. Brother Blair withdrew even more during these times of what he called *persecution*.

All He Wanted to Do Was Help

After we had been there several years, Blair created boards and appointed the board members. Blair appointed Curtis as chairman of the finance board, though it was in name only. The only bank account Curtis was privy to was the one they used to pay the utility bills and other non-ministerial expenses. Curtis had no knowledge of the salaries of any of the ministers. Blair had all the authority and made all the decisions, and because of some of the unwise demands he made, he seemed to lack any concept of business or finance. Neither did he trust any member to advise him. Instead, Curtis's role was to come up with the money for Blair's projects. This added stress to Curtis and so to our family, but he would never think to complain about it. Curtis trusted Brother Blair and kept trying to believe everything he said.

Curtis had a busy law practice when we joined, but he wanted to use his expertise to help Homestead in every way he could. There are certain rules to running organizations like Homestead, and Curtis truly wanted it to succeed and avoid getting into trouble. He was the only lawyer in the group until 2004, plus he had been a CPA and worked for a large CPA firm for a few years before law school, so his legal and accounting expertise was invaluable to Brother Blair. Especially because it was all free. When Brother Blair wasn't writing what we called *the literature*, he was busy thinking about the yearly building project or acquiring land.

Brother Blair found some land he wanted to buy in Colorado. He said he wanted it as a "retreat" and directed Homestead to pay for it. Brother Howard signed the contract to buy the land before he asked Curtis to review it. Curtis noticed that the only access from a public road to the property was through a neighbor's property. Curtis warned Howard not to close on the purchase until the neighboring property owners signed a written access easement. Howard told Curtis that "The Lord said there wouldn't be an issue with the easement," so they closed on the purchase against Curtis's advice. The husband of one of the neighbors was an attorney who specialized in real estate litigation. When they told Homestead it was not allowed to drive through their property, Homestead sued. During the nine years of the litigation, the leaders directed their followers in many, many prayer meetings to pray for success in the lawsuit. When they finally lost the easement, I don't recall that the leaders ever notified the followers of the loss. Homestead spent more money on the fees for their Colorado attorneys in the easement dispute than they had spent to buy the land. The reason Blair wanted to buy that land was so he and his family could move there before the Great Tribulation.

There was no end to the need for legal services among the members who were starting and running businesses, buying land and houses or being sued by a disgruntled customer. Curtis knew some of the judges and lawyers in town and tried to be a liaison by using his reputation to speak of Homestead as a legitimate Christian organization.

Brother Blair had an aversion to government regulations. He didn't believe specialists like electricians and plumbers should have to qualify for state licenses. His goal for Homestead was to be self-sufficient in all areas of life. For him, the government was in the way in almost all areas that Homesteaders worked in.

For example, since the midwifery program was a *ministry,* Brother Blair never allowed the midwives to obtain licenses. Couples were not allowed to get state marriage licenses. In church meetings he spoke derogatorily of medical doctors who were referred to as specialists. He was thrilled when a General Practitioner joined the group, so he had the members build a medical clinic as his project one year. Brother Blair became increasingly more reclusive as the years went by, so the resident physician afforded him the luxury of having a doctor at his beck and call.

The ministers spent long hours discussing Brother Blair's plans to build a solar energy system where an elaborate series of descending lakes would generate electricity and the community land would not have to depend on the local power coop. Our outdated and rust-laden water wells would be replaced by our own water treatment plant. One year Brother Blair said God's will was to build a towering interpretive center where visitors would learn about the roots of Homestead in a museum-like space. Due to the current exorbitant debt, Curtis was having to arrange with banks in town for Homestead to borrow money just to pay the utility bills, so he had no idea how Brother Blair thought these elaborate projects would be funded. All of the mounting pressure Curtis felt to please Brother Blair and the conflict in Curtis's own heart about Blair's financial irresponsibility would come to a head soon enough.

My husband hates to borrow money. He worked hard and only spent money he had. We hardly ever bought new cars. I shopped at thrift stores. He bought a Chevy Aveo, and we were constantly mocked for driving such a cheap car. It got 45 miles to a gallon. I think Curtis was making a statement with that car. Brother Blair and his sons bought new expensive cars every couple of years.

When couples married at Homestead, the wives had trouble getting social security cards and drivers' licenses with their new names. Curtis asked why they weren't allowed to file for state marriage licenses.

Curtis questioned why the leaders made every father lie on their babies' birth certificates. The fathers weren't allowed to say a midwife delivered their baby; they had to claim that the father delivered the baby on the birth certificate application.

When one of our grandbabies was stillborn, we wondered why the leaders didn't allow our grandbaby to be named. Brother Tzafrir told Curtis we weren't allowed to discuss the issue with our child; it wasn't *our place*. Because we questioned the leaders, they punished us by driving a wedge between us and our child. From then on, our relationship with our child eroded and because she was weak and vulnerable, she allowed the leaders to take our place. We were told our child and her husband no longer needed advice from us.

In order to help the community have clean water, Curtis asked the trustees if they would want him to buy our house (that we had paid to build) and some of Homestead's land (that we had bought for Homestead) to provide money to bring in water from the local water company. Blair approved the idea, and the trustees signed a written contract with Curtis in which Homestead agreed to use the money Curtis gave them to install water from Chalk Bluff Water Supply. Instead of using the money Curtis gave them to make the system legal, they breached their contract with Curtis and used the money for something else.

Curtis questioned why Homestead led the public to believe that the food served at the Cafe was organic and locally grown, when in fact almost all of it came from Sysco, Boar's Head, Ben E. Keith, and Sam's Club. In the end Curtis had a list of over 30 questions he wanted answers to. Curtis, being a loyal and devoted person, wanted clarity for Homestead's sake. He felt the leaders were treading on some shaky ground and could end up being sued. Curtis asked these questions for years without getting anywhere, the stress of what could happen constantly wearing on him. None of his questions were ever answered. Either Brother Blair's sons were afraid to ask their father about the issues or Brother Blair didn't care. Still, Curtis held out hope that one day

Brother Blair would listen, and they would get things straightened out, the debt paid off and Homestead on course.

Untethered from Reality

Warning to the reader: Some of the content of this chapter seems absolutely absurd; but I assure you it is all true.

This story begins, as many do, with an ordinary event, although in this case it was with an extraordinary person. A prominent business man, one of the wealthiest men in Waco, went to a chiropractor's office for an appointment. While in the waiting room, he noticed a hand-embroidered piece hanging on the wall. When he commented on the craftwork, a young woman from Homestead who was in the same waiting room told him that she had made it. I don't know whether the young woman had ever heard of the man or if the man had ever heard of Homestead Heritage at that point. A conversation ensued between the 90-ish-year-old man and the 20-ish year-old woman. Thus began the intense and intriguing saga that dominated our prayer meetings and the leaders' strange, "strategic" planning for the next four years.

The young lady reported back to the Homestead leadership about her fortuitous meeting at the chiropractor's office. One thing led to another and before you know it, the man had become so enamored with Homestead Heritage that he told the young lady he had decided to give nine billion dollars to her to do as she felt best. She told the leaders that she had met Bill Clinton and Nancy Pelosi at the rich man's home and that she would be invited to speak at her new friend's funeral when that time came. After other discussions, he clarified that he did not want to give the money directly to the group since it professed to be Christian.

But he would give it to his new young friend. The Homestead leaders knew the young lady would hand the money over to them so they could do God's work with it. The focus of what to do with all of the nine billion dollars absorbed all the leaders' time. Blair warned that a gift of that magnitude would surely corrupt all he had sacrificed for, so he devised a plan to start a new entity to receive the gift, an educational entity, and he began an initiative to buy land everywhere. These satellite communities would spread the Kingdom of God all over the world. Blair's dream was coming true. This belief that Homestead would be overflowing with cash set the stage for a situation that affected Curtis and me for the next six years.

Sometimes people ask me if you are required to give everything you own to Homestead when you join. Just like the *unspoken patterns* I talked about earlier, Blair would never say it was a requirement to give up your wealth. The message at many meetings was that God's will required us to sacrifice everything. Each listener had to make a choice about what to sacrifice. Curtis started out trying to help the Fellowship out by bailing them out of debt in Colorado so the group would not go bankrupt. We thought we were giving our money for God's work, even though we knew Blair had made some very irresponsible decisions. His modus operandi was to declare that God had spoken to him concerning buying land somewhere or starting an expensive project, and then expect the members to come up with the money. He used Scriptures like the rich young ruler in Matthew 19:16-30, or in Luke 14:25-33 that says that anyone who does not renounce all that he has cannot be Jesus' disciple. Since Blair put all his followers under a load of condemnation already, these tactics made us feel like we were not doing enough.

After we had bailed the Fellowship out of their debt in Colorado where they had bought the ranch they named Rehoboth and then bought the farm in Waco for them, my parents were afraid that in our zeal we'd give all of my inheritance to the group. Using wisdom, they put everything I was to inherit from them in a trust fund that I could not by law give away. Brother Tzafrir told someone who asked where we got our money that we had won the lottery. Neither Curtis nor I have ever bought a lottery ticket. Later Howard said my dad was a gambler! No one who knew my dad would agree with that. He grew up poor. His father worked two jobs to support his family. My dad drilled into me to never borrow anything from anyone and to only buy what I had the money for. Regina met my kind and funny dad one time and she told me he was the strangest man she'd ever met! Those negative, condescending comments were the framework of the community. They built Homestead up at the expense of tearing everyone else outside of them down. Regina wanted me to extract myself from my blood family because now, she and the rest of the Homestead members were my real family. As Blair would say in many a meeting, *If anyone comes to me and does not hate his own father and mother and wife and children and brothers and sisters, yes, and even his own life, he cannot be my disciple. Luke 14:26 (ESV)* Another verse he often quoted was *Mark 3:33-35(ESV), And he answered them, 'Who are my mother and my brothers?' And looking about at those who sat around him, he said 'Here are my mother and my brothers! For whoever does the will of God he is my brother and sister and mother.'* Blair believed he was the center of God's will and those of us who put him above our own families were the true disciples on the earth.

Blair constantly planned for the ultimate place of refuge for himself and his family during the great tribulation. While we were members, Homestead had bought numerous pieces of land and each purchase was preceded by Blair prophesying that it was God's will. Before Blair had bought the land with the easement issue in Colorado, he bought a ranch in New Mexico that had terrible roads and were too difficult for Blair's family to get to. The altitude at ten thousand feet at another large tract in Colorado gave Blair altitude sickness along with high blood pressure so he only went there a few times, then they sold it.

He insisted on buying a cattle ranch in Oklahoma. The cattle operation resulted in a huge financial failure and became a money pit.

In 2008 Blair was certain the nine billion would be his any day, so while some of his trusted leaders were scouting out land for new communities, he sent others off in all directions to search for another personal refuge for him and his family. He found what he deemed God's will in Deary, Idaho. There were three buildings on the land. We called one the bunk house, another the main house, and the third was a cabin on the beautiful Potlatch River. The main house featured eight bedrooms because the people who built it had a large family.

I remember the night Curtis came home from a ministers' meeting where Blair said that God had spoken to him audibly that the land in Deary would be his. What Curtis said next undid me. He said he had committed to use the trust money to buy the land. I wondered if we'd ever see that money again. Curtis said the trust would own the land and Homestead would pay rent to the trust until they could buy it. The Homestead elders promised that they would buy the land from the trust within six months. I had watched the Homestead leadership make poor decisions that led to more and more debt, and deep inside I didn't think they were trustworthy. Curtis agreed they continuously squandered the gifts people gave them and grew more stressed as the debt rose, but he kept trying to help them. He believed they would eventually listen to him. After all, we had given up everything because we wanted the dream of close community to come true. So I swallowed hard and put on a happy face.

Aber had a contract drawn up that stated they would buy back the Idaho land ASAP. He enthusiastically stated verbally they would buy the land back within six months because his father heard from God that the nine-billion-dollar gift would fall into his lap soon. The written agreement said they would pay us a certain amount of rent each month. We received the first month's rent and never heard another word from

Aber about the rent for three years. Blair prophesied he was going to own the land in Idaho, but what he hadn't heard from the Lord was there would be an economic crash that same year! Lehman Brothers, the prominent global financial investment bank went bankrupt two weeks before closing on the purchase of the land in Idaho. The Café and Craft Village sales went way down along with most members' businesses.

A family from Texas had been sent to live on the property in Idaho and take care of it for the Adamses. They moved their large family into the main house. They found out that the entire Adams family planned to spend the summer in Idaho. Aber informed them they would have to move their family into the bunk house for the summer. This was no small task and caused a lot of grief for the mother of ten to pack up and move out. They were required to do this every summer. Each year the mother developed a bad attitude toward the Adamses, and I was given the task to *minister* to her. Aber's wife instructed me that this family was on the verge of being sent home to Texas and possibly disfellowshipped if the mother didn't repent. I wondered what my attitude would have been if I had to move out of my house and into that rough bunk house every summer. But I obeyed and talked to her even though I had no first-hand knowledge of what was really going on. I just had enough sense to know that this mom needed to shape up and pledge her loyalty to Blair. That was the solution to all our problems.

After the family moved in and out of the bunkhouse several times, they were given permission to build a new house for their family on the property. They were going to bulldoze the two-story bunkhouse and build a new house in the same location. But the local building code required a building permit. Blair hated to comply with "worldly" laws. So they decided rather than build a new house they would "remodel" the old one. They "remodeled" it by tearing down all of the bunk house except one small part of the foundation. The trust my parents created owned the property and even though they knew Curtis was the trustee, no one thought to tell Curtis about it. He didn't find out about the project until it was well under way. He was mad no one had thought to tell him about it. The what's yours is mine *pattern* took precedence like usual. Curtis feared he'd be charged with a criminal violation of the local building code. While they were building the new house, Curtis asked Brother Tzafrir for permission to go to Idaho and see the project but was denied permission to go there! Later Curtis asked for permission again and Tzafrir said we could go for three days. It's a day's travel time to and from Texas to Idaho so that seemed impractical. Regina invited us to visit for her birthday one time and we looked forward to finally being able to see the land. A few days before we were to leave Tzafrir called and said it wasn't a good time for us to go after all.

As a result of the Deary community complaining about what they called a strange group possibly being a cult moving into their tight knit community, the Homestead leaders met with the Deary community leaders and citizens to explain what their intentions were there. Aber told them they were not a church, but a school called Ploughshare. That was news to all of us who had never heard that before! We had been told Blair wanted to start another community there. To us that meant he intended to start a satellite church community. No matter what the current name of the group was, it was always called *the church.* We had been taught to uphold the reputation Blair had built. It seemed to me he was using deception to get his way in the Deary community. We bit our tongues and kept quiet.

Curtis kept the pressure on Aber to pay back the purchase price of the land in Idaho and after one rent payment in four years they deeded to the trust a small parcel of land they owned in Colorado as partial payment for the rent. Five years later they sold the Oklahoma ranch and we were excited they finally had the money to pay us back. My mother had died during this stressful time and Howard tried to pressure Curtis into forgiving the debt by saying my mother, whether she was in heaven or hell, would want to buy the land in Idaho for them. Cutis and I had fallen for a lot of their manipulation but we laughed at that one. Howard didn't know my mother at all. They reluctantly, but finally, paid us back for the Idaho land.

The rich man died in 2012. He hadn't given any money to Homestead before he died, so the leaders were certain that he left everything in his will to the young girl. But he didn't. We never heard another word about him.

The 501(d)

A huge test of Curtis's loyalty came when Howard told Curtis that Blair wanted to form a Section 501(d) organization. Most churches, schools and hospitals are tax-exempt under Section 501(c) of the Internal Revenue Code. Although Curtis had practiced tax accounting and law for years, he had never heard of Section 501(d) of the I. R. C., entitled "Apostolic and Religious Organizations." After he did some research, he found that only a handful of small entities, including a few convents and monasteries, claimed that tax status. The main tax advantage of a 501(d) is that the members are exempt from social security tax. Blair wanted all the money that the members would have otherwise been paying into social security. This was a big dream Blair had. At one time he said it was the most important decision he had ever made. Curtis didn't like the idea at all and dragged his feet in filing the form with the Internal Revenue Service until Howard told him to get it done. Since Brother Blair told the congregation it was the Lord's will for us to have a 501(d), that's what Curtis set up. Blair picked a real doosie of a name: "Koinonia Craftsmen, A Religious Order of the Brazos de Dios Koinonia Community." They later changed the name to Homestead Heritage.

The 501(d) started out slowly. But as Brother Blair preached that God wanted members of the church who owned businesses to donate their businesses to the 501(d) so they would be under "apostolic authority," more and more members did that. Although Blair didn't come out of the closet and officially declare himself to be an "apostle" until years later, everyone knew from the beginning of the 501(d) that he thought he was the apostle in the "apostolic organization." He named some brothers, including Curtis, as trustees, but none of them had any authority to do anything except what Blair wanted them to do. Blair frequently reiterated that the 501(d) was "the center of God's will." But some members of the church, including even some of the trustees, were reluctant to turn over ownership of their businesses to the 501(d). Curtis never put his law practice in it, but after the first man Blair named as president left Homestead, Blair appointed Curtis president. He wanted to take advantage of Curtis's good reputation in the world outside Homestead. That's what caused the pressure on Curtis. The members of the group erroneously thought Curtis had some authority in the entity. He had none. Blair put all the responsibility on Curtis, but gave him no authority. He was told that he was not allowed to participate in any hiring, firing, or any other personnel decision, or make any business decisions concerning any of the businesses in the 501(d). His only duty was to borrow enough money to keep it afloat.

Governor George W. and Laura Bush hired Homestead Heritage, the 501(d), to build a house on their ranch near Waco. That gave the group notoriety, and more members of Homestead gave their businesses to Blair's apostolic 501(d). Our oldest son worked on the construction of the Bushes' house. He has the privilege of saying that he was in the president's cabinet. (He has a picture of himself standing inside one of the cabinets that he helped build in the president's library.)

Since I am not an expert on the tax code or anything close to it, my summary here might not be accurate according to all the laws. (I don't even pay the bills). This is just my memory of the twenty years the 501(d) dominated our lives. The phrase 501(d) was such a big part of our lives that when I bought my boys' jeans, they asked if I had gotten them Levi's 501(d)'s!

Brother Blair's goal was to model Homestead on Marx's idea of communism: "From each according to his ability, to each according to his need." Through his preaching, Blair put pressure on all the business owners to turn their businesses over to the 501(d) entity. They were to declare how much money they would need to live on each month and leave the leftover profits in the general fund. The goal was for that money to pay for Brother Blair's yearly project goals, which always included a new building project. All the boys and men were urged to work on those building projects without compensation, in addition to their regular jobs. I don't know if any of the profits went to help the widows, indigent or sick. Most members who were business owners complained, but signed over their businesses to Homestead's 501(d). Those members who resisted the change of their business status were hounded by the ministers for years. I remember hearing about one brother who owned a profitable construction business in Austin who refused--and for good reason. He had the foresight to predict the outcome of that decision. We can look at Cuba for example or Russia or any other country controlled by communism. It leads to poverty, starvation, and rebellion. On a much smaller scale, Homestead also became an example of the consequences of an idyllic collective. It sounded good in theory, especially to the impoverished, which a lot of the working class at Homestead were, but it didn't work any better there than it has anywhere else on earth.

The men who donated their businesses to the 501(d) were expected to continue managing them. Not only their profit motive but also their authority over their businesses was taken away from them. The elders of the church were the "covering" of the 501(d). (Curtis was never on the board of elders of Homestead. He was never even told who the members of the board of elders were.) Creativity among the former business owners was squelched because they no longer had the freedom to run their businesses as they thought fit. The leaders breathed down their necks to work harder and make more money for "God's Kingdom."

One by one each business became less profitable. Interestingly, the one that refused to succumb to Blair's wishes thrived. Fear always snuffs out creativity, and the dogmatic control and scrutiny of the leaders who had very little business sense or experience caused fear to replace creativity. It seems obvious now, and yet then, none of the leaders understood what was happening until it was too late. Profits went way down and there never was enough money to go around. The former business owners were asked to take even less, and this put strain on the families who were already having a hard time making ends meet.

Each time Blair told his son Aber to build a new building, Aber would tell Curtis what his dad wanted, and Curtis would respond that they would have to borrow the money to build it. Unfazed about not having any money, Aber instructed Curtis to borrow the money, time after time after time.

Prosperity became an ongoing dilemma at Homestead. One Sunday, the young people were brow-beaten to take initiative. When they did take initiative and began to be successful, they would be "ministered" to about making too much money and going to hell. It seemed most of the young people were too afraid to take initiative since they had learned the hard way what the consequences were for what the leadership deemed *getting ahead of God*. If they made money and bought a nice truck, they'd *get in trouble* for being "worldly." The leadership never struck a happy medium and fear remained the common denominator. Some young people who were particularly close to the founder's family were exceptions and were exempt from scrutiny; everyone else was fair game.

Brother Blair hated bad news. He always said anything bad that happened at Homestead was the enemy attacking him personally. So, the elders had a hard time giving Brother Blair any news that wasn't good, especially if it involved the failure of one of his "visions." Since he firmly believed all of his ideas were the will of God, he could not be wrong. So he publicly rebuked the men who had laid their formerly profitable businesses at his feet. Like Pharaoh ordered the Israelites, Blair told the members of the 501(d), "Work harder and faster with fewer resources!"

When things got so desperate that the 501(d) did not have enough money to pay the payroll, Aber told Curtis to borrow the money to pay it. The next payroll he got the same message. "Borrow more money to cover payroll." And the next payroll. Three payrolls in a row. Curtis's little log office sat across the road from our house. I'd watch him pacing back and forth on the front porch. His stress level soared and carried over to our home life. He was short with the kids and me as the years went on, and because of it I became stressed and yelled at the kids more. His stress stemmed from helplessness. He held the title of chairman of the finance board, but in reality he had absolutely no authority to do anything other than what he was told to do.

While money dwindled and the businesses failed, Brother Blair kept right on dreaming up new projects. Expensive projects that he expected Curtis to find the money to fund. By this time Aber, who had never worked outside the group, would tell Curtis to "just come up with the money." My husband is the most loyal person I know, and he had given everything he had to support this group, but the disparity between reality and Brother Blair's so called "vision" and "kingdom of God" caused such conflict in his heart and mind I thought he might crack under the pressure. I was on the verge myself just watching the drama play out. No one in leadership cared about Curtis's mounting physical and emotional strain any more than they cared for the 501(d) members' personal situations.

Brother Blair's sons and Brother Howard were desperate to please the one they had pledged their lives to serve, so anyone beneath them was expected to do whatever it took to keep him happy, regardless of any obstacles. The financial situation became so dire that finally Homestead's bank even refused to lend the group the coins it needed for change for its annual craft fair, even though they had always paid back the money they borrowed for change after the first day of the fair. In spite of Homestead's fading reputation at the banks, the leaders still demanded Curtis to bail out the bankrupt 501(d) and fund more projects. Every month Curtis sent Brother Blair along with another elder and his son the bleak financial reports sounding the alarm that Homestead's debt was mounting into the millions, but no one listened. Aber finally told Curtis that his father told him to stop sending him financial reports. Aber said he'd give the reports to Blair himself. (Aber later confirmed he had kept his father continuously updated on the increasingly bleak financial situation.)

In December of 2010 Homestead was on the verge of bankruptcy. Blair called a church-wide meeting where he stood in front of the congregation and said he had just been informed that the church was in four and a half million dollars of debt, and without using Curtis's name he implied it was Curtis's fault. Curtis had been sounding the alarm about the mounting debt for years! Brother Blair, who Curtis had given his time, talents, and resources to, lied to a thousand people and turned his back on one of his most loyal followers.

The next month Blair announced that it was God's will for the brothers who had donated their businesses to his apostolic organization to now buy their businesses back. They each had to borrow the money to buy their own businesses from Blair's apostolic "order." Blair got out of debt by having his brothers (followers) borrow the money personally. Homestead Heritage, the 501(d) was dissolved.

Black Friday

In 2012 Brother Blair announced Homestead had "lost favor" in Waco and needed to relocate. This was not the first time. They were run out of Colorado in the 80's and ended up moving the group to Austin and then to Waco. Since the 90's very few people living in the Waco area had joined the community. The café was losing money every month, and the group wasn't growing. Brother Blair proposed several schemes to remedy the situation. One plan was that seventy percent of the members would scatter outside of Texas. Only a skeleton crew would stay in Waco which would be home base for all new communities. All new recruits would be sent to Waco for training in the patterns and doctrine. In meeting after meeting, the leaders exhorted us to obey God and scatter. They said if we didn't, we would lose everything because of our disobedience, reminding us that God's timing is everything. Everyone began talking about places where they felt led to move. One older minister said he wanted his entire small group to move to Missouri. Brother Blair proposed that a core group of 200 people including the entire church office and everyone who worked on publishing his books should all move to Boise, Idaho -- in a month!

(As usual), people began having dreams. A lot of the dreams were about specific places to start new communities. Brother Blair's daughter dramatically relayed one she had about two houses. One house was dilapidated and many people tried to repair it, but it couldn't be fixed. The house kept falling apart. The other house was well built and beautiful. According to Brother Blair the first house represented the Waco community and the second house represented God's blessings of our obedience. He used this dream to reiterate that we had to scatter before it was too late.

Curtis and I were excited about hearing from God and doing His will. We prayed God would show us where He wanted to plant a new community and whether we were supposed to move or not. When we felt we heard God say, "Virginia," several others said they felt the same. Curtis wrote a letter to Brother Blair saying we felt led to look for land in Virginia for a potential new community. The letter didn't say anything about our moving there right away. Curtis had just moved his parents to Waco. His dad was very sick at the time and we spent a great deal of our time helping his parents, so we didn't think we'd be moving anywhere for a long time.

Curtis talked to his two ministers, Howard and Tzafrir, about the letter in November 2012 before the annual Thanksgiving Craft Fair. Their only comment to Curtis was that he should wait for the "right" time to give it to Blair. Everybody was busy for weeks preparing for the Fair. The group rarely had church meetings from mid-September until mid-January to prepare for the Fair and the Christmas program and recuperate afterwards.

Our first Sunday meeting in 2013 was on January 20. That Sunday Blair preached again on the necessity of scattering. He told the story of when they relocated from New York to Colorado no one talked to anyone other than Blair about where they were feeling led to move. The next day Curtis gave his letter to Aber to give to Blair. Curtis thought that was the "right time" he'd been waiting for.

We assumed Brother Blair would be pleased when he read Curtis's letter. But on January 25, 2013, our lives drastically and abruptly changed course. Our family refers to this date as Black Friday.

Black Friday Meeting

Instead of being pleased with our obedience, Blair instructed his ministers to press in and find the real reason Curtis wrote the letter. Howard called Curtis that night to tell him that the letter was not God's will. Curtis didn't sleep much that week and was ordered to the conference room at all hours of the day and night. The ministers spent most of these sessions rejecting Curtis' reason for writing the letter to Brother Blair. Curtis insisted he was obeying Blair's call to scatter, but Howard and Tzafrir kept insisting he dig to the root of his "rebellion."

This "ministry" was considered the normal method the ministers used to get a confession out of the "accused." Remember, at Homestead everything was investigated. Brother Blair never attended these discipline sessions but spoke to Curtis through Brother Howard and Brother Tzafrir. In fact, even though Curtis was one of his most loyal followers, Blair never had a single private conversation with Curtis in person. Curtis spent most of the next four days in the conference room where the ministers repeatedly reminded him that his heart was deceitfully wicked and he needed them, the ministers, to help him see his rebellious heart. The sleepless nights and anxiety-riddled days where he was told his salvation hung in the balance took its toll physically, mentally, and emotionally. Once he was worn down, the ministers told him what Brother Blair said was Curtis's real issue: he wanted to move to Virginia in order to get away from Blair. Brother Howard accused Curtis of dishonoring Blair and not trusting him anymore. After all, Curtis had questioned the debt and Blair's repeated decisions to borrow more and more money. On top of that, the ministers blamed Curtis for an ailment Sister Regina had at the time. According to Homestead beliefs, his "sin" had opened the door to the enemy and was the root cause of her affliction. The remedy was for Curtis to admit he had sinned and recommit his unfailing trust in and loyalty to Brother Blair and his leadership. Then he could possibly prove his loyalty and come back into Brother Blair's good graces.

Curtis was confused. He couldn't see how he had been disloyal or dishonoring; he had followed all the "patterns" and he had literally given everything to this group and sacrificed his time and energy for their benefit for decades. We had clung to the hope that we had given up everything so that our family could live the wholesome simple life Homestead had promised and offer that hope to the world.

On Friday, January 25, 2013, there was a call for a mandatory church-wide meeting. That same afternoon Curtis came home from a meeting in the conference room exhausted. My heart broke at seeing him. The mental and emotional torture of explaining himself all week had taken its toll. I knew something was wrong. He told me that afternoon he had caved in and told them that Blair was right. He said, "I have been lying on the floor of the conference room for 45 minutes, begging for forgiveness." Curtis said the ministers had told him, "It was never God's will for you and your family to move to Virginia. Your heart has deceived you." Curtis told them it was 99% his fault, but Howard retorted, "It's not 99% your fault. It's 100% your fault!" As part of his penance, Tzafrir told Curtis to apologize for his letter and read a Scripture at the special, mandatory meeting that night. Curtis would speak before Blair shared an "important" message with the church.

That evening, we went to the dreaded meeting thinking the crisis was over. Curtis apologized and shared the approved Scripture. When Brother Blair stood to relay his important message, he hesitated and then exclaimed, "I don't feel any repentance in Curtis's testimony." As he spoke, his voice grew louder and louder until he was yelling, ranting and raving about disfellowshipping Curtis. In his rant, he yelled into the microphone, "The *brothers* have gone to Curtis twice about this issue and he refused to listen!" In other words, "I am following Matthew 18 about kicking an unrepentant person out of the church!" Blair told the congregation that Curtis's sin was dishonor. He had not followed the pattern of going to the ministers. He had dishonored Blair by sending the letter directly to Blair.

My body shut down. I kept thinking over and over again: What was he ranting about? What had Curtis done wrong? He had repented, told the ministers they were right and had read the Scripture as instructed. All hope of forgetting the past week was shattered. The room was so quiet I thought I could hear my heart pounding.

One young man warily stood and tried to confess some sin, but was told, "Sit down. Curtis is on trial, and everyone is to learn from his sin."

Over the years I had witnessed Brother Blair spewing out his wrath on many people and wondered when we'd be singled out and be the brunt of his rage. Now that it was here, it seemed like the worst of all rebukes. My mouth turned dry and I shook from head to toe.

Somehow, I managed to stand up and say, "I have been tempted to pick up my coat and run out of the building, but I know we have to face the storm."

Then I sat down, humiliated, and afraid to look anyone in the eye. I really didn't know what to do with myself. I felt like I was suffocating, and I wasn't sure I wanted to come up for air.

The Aftermath of Brother Blair's Rage

The next day I was lying in bed staring at the ceiling when Sister Regina called me and said, "It's beyond emotion, isn't it?"

Precisely. I was beyond emotion. I couldn't cry or feel anything. I was traumatized. I tried to act normal, like nothing had happened, but that day I had my first panic attack. From then on for two years, I lived from one panic attack to another. For three years after that I lived with extreme anxiety. That horrific night severed my identity. I was doomed to be a nobody. I became an outcast among this group of people I had pledged my life to and they to me. I had always tried to make people happy, but now it seemed to me everyone was upset with me. Rejection was my worst fear, and it had now become my reality.

Curtis and I became pariahs overnight. People avoided us. They were too afraid they'd get in trouble if they talked to us. It was like someone had died and everyone was at a loss for words. I couldn't sleep or eat much so I spent many nights on my face in the living room begging God to forgive me. And I felt like it was all my fault. Maybe I finally agreed with the leaders that the woman was always suspect because Eve ate the apple first.

I thought confessing would bring some sort of relief, so at a meeting in the conference room, I told Brother Tzafrir and Brother Howard it was all my fault. I explained that since Curtis had been the chairman of the finance board, his stress level had skyrocketed, and all that stress had taken a toll on our family. I tried to help the leaders see that as the Homestead debt rose to 4 ½ million dollars, Curtis, who hated debt and had used his name as good faith at the banks in town, was worried. I told them he would be shocked when on many occasions he learned that Brother Blair had started another expensive building project. When Curtis asked how they expected to pay for the project, the standard answer was, "That's your job. Just borrow the money."

When I mentioned the word *stress,* Brother Tzafrir mocked me. He sneered and said, "You felt stress! You poor thing!"

He continued condescendingly interjecting the word *stress* throughout the meeting. I confessed my failure to trust the leaders after they breached their contract to pay my trust back for the Idaho land. They didn't seem to care what we thought or felt. We were to keep on trusting even when they failed to keep their end of the bargain. Debt didn't seem to bother them; they would just whip the slaves harder to sacrifice more time and money.

In my confession session with the leaders, I told them I wanted people to like me and now it felt like everyone was mad at me. I was so stressed I even confessed that I voted for myself for "Most Popular" in my senior class. There were only 36 of us! I liked people, I told them, and needed them.

The leaders decided I needed some "alone time." So from then on, I wasn't invited to the fellowships, birthdays, or showers that had defined our lives. Friends would say they didn't see me at some occasion where they expected me to be, and I realized I hadn't been invited. Or I'd hear someone talking about an event I was excluded from and my loneliness skyrocketed. We had been blacklisted overnight.

I knew if I talked to anyone about what I felt, all hell would break loose. The leaders mocked psychology or counseling just as they did Trinitarians, (those who were baptized in the name of the Father, Son and Holy Ghost-- as Jesus commanded), and even others who were baptized in "Jesus' name only," but weren't under the authority of Homestead leaders. Their cure for everything was to trust in the leader's vision and willingly sacrifice your life. They believed that all depression and anxiety resulted from not being properly submitted to the leaders of Homestead. They taught that if I could ever get to the bottom of the hidden sin in my deceitful heart, I could be set free. I believed this teaching. I endured the next five years hiding pain and fear and pretending that I was okay.

Shortly after Black Friday, I had my annual birthday breakfast with my best friend, Sister Regina. Or should I say, my best friend before Black Friday. She had taken me to breakfast for my birthday for years, which was considered a great honor at Homestead. She told me on more than one occasion that she only did that with her oldest granddaughter and me.

I went to that breakfast hoping for some compassion or hope. I was weary and racked with anxiety and in need of love. Soon after we ordered our food, she informed me that Curtis and I would no longer be in the "inner circle." I had never heard anyone at Homestead talk about an inner circle. Curtis and I had never thought about being in an inner circle. The point of the breakfast was to end our relationship. That was my last birthday breakfast with her.

For days I thought about our conversation. She had mentioned me not being in the inner circle, but this confused me. What was the inner circle and why did we have one? Who was in this inner circle? Even if I didn't understand everything, I got the general message: we had failed beyond any remedy.

This left me without love and without hope. The person I considered my best friend and mentor made clear we were no longer friends. My life began swirling down a black vortex. I had lost everything I had trusted in. Our so-called *place,* and the friends we had committed to, were stripped away. Nightmares about being kicked out of the inner circle became a common occurrence. I constantly asked God to forgive me. Guilt became an unbearable, constant burden. My life began to unravel, and I was completely helpless to stop it. I had trusted and believed the founder. We taught our children to honor him. If asked, they would say they believed at one time he was like God.

For months after Black Friday, it seemed many Sunday meetings were directed at Curtis and me. At one, Blair had his son-in-law quote the divorce statistics in the U.S. and then quote the divorce statistics among those who leave Homestead, and then repeat the line we heard so often, "We've never had a divorce at Homestead." (As long as you remain a member you cannot get divorced. There have been plenty who have left and divorced.)

This was a line they used to convince visitors that Homestead was Nirvana. The founder's voice grew louder and louder until the crescendo, "You're going to get divorced if you leave!"

The realization hit me hard. Not that we'd get divorced. Instead, it was as though my eyes were opened to seeing how Blair used his outbursts of anger to manipulate the congregation. He used fear to paralyze us so we wouldn't leave his kingdom! Fear, shame, and blame kept us rooted in condemnation which kept us at Homestead. Blair had repeatedly told us that Homestead was the kingdom of God. That day I asked myself, "Where is the peace, love, and joy in the Holy Spirit that the Bible says is the Kingdom of God?"

When the meeting was finally over, I walked down the aisle to exit the building and locked eyes with one of my daughters. She looked alarmed, afraid we would leave Homestead, but because of the snitching culture we lived in, I couldn't talk to her without knowing she'd feel obligated, and maybe a little elated, to *tattle*.

Curtis, who thrived on lots of activity, had lost what they called his "place" and found himself trying to get re-oriented. He was not about to leave Homestead. He had signed his name to the life-long pledge and would never consider going back on his word. He had time to take craft classes. He signed up for pottery, gardening, and cheese classes. He even made a guitar. Next, he decided to renovate the log home where we'd raised our nine children.

Curtis hoped Blair had erroneously accused him of not first going to Howard or Tzafrir about his letter. Curtis suspected that Howard and Tzafrir had not had the courage to admit to Blair that Curtis had in fact talked with them first. Curtis also knew God wanted him to forgive them all. So he did. He hoped those men would humble themselves and apologize. They never did.

I couldn't tell anyone what was happening in my life for fear of repercussions of more shame and blame. The one time I mentioned slightly off-handedly that I was struggling to a supposed close friend, Curtis received a call from Howard who told him, "Get your wife in line!" No one in that group, which the leaders touted to be the center of God's will on the earth, had any wisdom, love, or comfort for me. I felt utterly alone and rejected. I didn't think hell could be worse. Curtis would hold me and pray for me.

I started neglecting my kids; their school was nonexistent. I remember telling my youngest daughter to figure it out on her own. I couldn't write a coherent sentence. When I tried to express what was going on or write a note, there was no connection between my brain and my hand. Everything seemed scrambled, like something was broken. I willed myself out of bed in the mornings. I hated having to wake up. Church meetings became torture. If we had to go to a mandatory church-wide meeting on Sunday or for an emergency prayer meeting in the sanctuary christened, Santa Fé Hall, I forced my feet to take each step. I hated who I was. I had heard how kids cut themselves and now I realized why. Self-hatred. I felt isolated and wished I would die. This death wish settled inside my mind, and it followed me daily.

I no longer knew if God really cared about me or if He really was who I had once believed. My salvation hung on by a thin thread, and my faith in God that I'd clung to most of my life slowly dwindled away. I began to believe that if God really didn't forgive our sins but kept a record of wrongs like the leaders did, and if there really isn't grace and love, then I didn't want anything to do with Him. The teaching Blair had pounded into us that there was no such thing as "once saved, always saved" became a reality for me. I felt completely abandoned and so far from God that I believed I had fallen beyond hope.

One night as I was leaving a prayer meeting, Regina stopped me and gestured with her hand moving from side to side, like she was sprinkling seeds. She told me to *spread faith here and there* and walked off. Her intention was to encourage me to perform so I could possibly work my way back into her good graces. It felt like she was throwing salt into a wound. My only hope there was to prove myself worthy of their approval. I didn't have that in me anymore. I realized I had been worshiping her and her husband, and for what? To be in the inner circle and feel good about myself? I had trusted them and believed them as if they were God.

After a Friday night meeting, Brother Howard told Curtis and me that he wanted to talk to us. Someone had a dream we were moving back to Dallas which worried all the leaders. Brother Howard talked to Curtis about him losing his *place* in the church and what a tragedy that was. He didn't say much about what was in the dream the member had about us except that in it we had a fancy chandelier and a big mantle that was too heavy to move. After speaking with us, Brother Howard came over to our house several times unannounced and walked around looking at our remodeling project. We were enclosing our porch. Every time he came, he seemed to be looking for something. It made me paranoid to the point that I worried my new chairs were too "worldly." I was terrified of getting into more trouble. It turned out he was looking to see if we were going to replace our non-electric candelabra with an electric chandelier. According to the dream, if we did get an electric chandelier, that meant we were going back to Dallas. Next we got a beige couch which also, according to the dream, meant we were leaving Homestead and moving back to Dallas.

This all made me want to move back to Dallas.

Joe and Max go to Camp and Horses take Joe to Israel

Max was 16 when our family made friends with an older couple outside of Homestead. They were longtime horse people and encouraged Max to start a trail riding business on our ranch. A couple Max knew in the Fellowship went horseback riding in Tennessee on their honeymoon. The man who owned the riding facility in Tennessee came for a visit and met Max who asked this man's advice about starting a horseback riding business. Max's new friend said he'd sell him seven Tennessee Walkers and throw in the tack.

Max's big brother, Joe, our fourth, was born with a business mind. He was never particularly fond of horses, but when Max pitched the idea to him, he went all in. Two years before Black Friday Joe purchased the horses, Max built a barn on the river bank, and they employed all able-bodied siblings and friends to help clear trails along the river and through the woods and ravines.

They named the business Brazos Bluffs Stables.

The trail riding business began as Joe's part-time job in 2010. When a customer called, Max or Joe saddled the horses, greeted the customers, went over safety instructions, and led the ride. If there were a lot of riders, he'd rustle up any available siblings to help, regardless of their riding abilities. On one memorable trail ride, one of his sisters rode a huge 30 year-old mule named Junior bareback. It was a hot summer day, and she wore her usual heavy denim jumper and a huge hat. Rather than staying on the marked trail, she led the group through the river so the horses and riders could cool off. That was not the trail they usually took. Soaking wet, she led the group up a steep trail, where she slid right off the back of Junior. She clambered back on only to slide off again on the next hill. One of the riders, a six-year-old boy, took note of his guide and asked his mother, "Does that lady know how to ride a horse?"

The Sheltered Cowboys Meet the World

A few days after the Brazos Bluffs Ranch website went live, Joe received a call from a lady on staff at a Jewish camp. She asked if he would supply the horses for their horseback riding program. Though he said no the first few times she asked, Joe eventually agreed to meet her at the camp and see the situation first-hand. After that meeting, Joe bought a horse trailer. On the first day of camp, Joe and his brother unloaded the horses and ate lunch in the noisy dining hall with two staff members, Michelle and Karen. Michelle and Karen sized up the boys quickly, "They weren't from around them parts."

Dressed in long-sleeved western shirts and cowboy hats, the boys were a stark contrast to the hundreds of gregarious kids at the other tables. My kids hadn't spoken a word. Karen, wanting them to feel at home, leaned over and asked, "Do y'all like Tractor Supply?" They stared at her a minute before Joe responded, "That's like my least favorite store." That warm welcome opened a whole new world to these sheltered cowboys.

Michelle included the boys in camp functions like Shabbat services on Friday night. They helped her in the camp garden and in the art room. She taught them how to tie-dye a t-shirt and make lanyards and stained glass. The boys learned a little Hebrew and grew accustomed to the Jewish songs, prayers, and blessings before, during, and after meals. Too shy and afraid they would get into trouble with the Homestead leaders, they watched while the campers and counselors danced Jewish dances. Those hot summer days at camp gave our kids a broader view of life. Besides all the campers from Texas and other states, dozens of young Israeli soldiers made up part of the staff. Joe and Max made lots of friends from Israel and all over Texas. Even though they grew tired of saddling, unsaddling, and hauling sweaty horses all summer, they loved being included in the Fourth of July fireworks, Shabbat dinners, and Israeli dancing afterwards.

Over the years that our boys were involved with the Jewish camp, we had invited the counselors to our house on the weekends they had off. Our girls would make them homemade meals, a welcome change from camp food. Our kids made scores of Israeli friends that they still keep up with. Because of our kids' work at camp, Curtis and I were sometimes invited to Shabat dinner on Friday nights. The relationships our kids made resulted in our hosting some of the Israelis' visiting parents. Because Max's birthday coincided with the end of camp, our kids invited all their new and old friends to attend his birthday party every year. Held at our pavilion by the Brazos River, these were fun evenings, with Ranger rides to the bluff, kids jamming on the deck, and tight-rope walking on a strap strung between a car bumper and pecan tree. Some campers sang songs like "California Dreaming" while drifting down the river in a canoe or kayak. This celebration became a tradition in our family for 10 years.

As soon as the Homestead leaders learned the camp was a Jewish camp and employed dozens of Israeli soldiers during the summer, they saw this as God's fertile field, "ripe for the harvest." Brother Blair's ultimate dream had been to start a community in Israel. He felt that was the fulfillment of prophecy. His vision would be the fulfillment of bringing the Jews to Christ. Because of that, Brother Tzafrir organized field trips to Homestead for the campers where they'd make crafts, watch demonstrations, and end the day with homemade ice cream.

This was before Black Friday, but after the pivotal meeting in 2010 about the large debt Homestead was in. Since that meeting, Curtis had been ostracized by the leadership. Blair had appointed Curtis as chairman of three of the church boards. There was no formal communication that he was no longer the chairman. Silence was the result of all the years Curtis had tried to serve them. In 2011they just stopped notifying him when the boards were meeting. When he had confronted Brother Blair (via his sons) about numerous legal issues and received the silent treatment, now his termination on all the boards was communicated the same way. After not being notified of any of the meetings, he deduced the obvious. They no longer wanted him. Curtis said in reality the boards were all a board of one anyway. Curtis wrote a written resignation from all the boards in 2013. It was his turn to feel Brother Blair's wrath as all the other leaders had over the years when he exalted those who honored his order without question and humiliated those who questioned. Curtis's frequent alarm sounding about the debt fell into the questioning category. The extent of Curtis's humbling extended to every aspect of our lives. Members were afraid to call him for advice for fear it would displease the ministers. We all felt put down when we were no longer worthy of participating in camp activities.

The opportunity to fulfill Brother Blair's vision in Israel had fallen into Brother Tzafrir's lap and this was his time to shine. Tzafrir replaced Joe and Max's staff with those who he thought were more "spiritual" trail guides, and he stationed those he deemed worthy at all camp functions, continually pushing our family out of the picture. It didn't matter that this was Joe's business or that the camp had hired Joe and Max to run the horseback program, not Tzafrir. Tzafrir wanted Joe and Max to provide the horses and the manpower, but forgo the friendships with the Israelis. I felt like we were in the military where certain ones were moving up in rank and we were waiting to be court-martialed unfairly.

Our family quickly realized that Tzafrir wanted us to move out of the way and let him take control of the camp. He made it clear that our kids had fulfilled their role in God's plan by providentially making contact with the camp, but their role was over. We were told Joe and his siblings were not spiritual enough to help these Jewish people. Brother Tzafrir would decide what kids would take their places at the camp. We got the hint loud and clear when Brother Blair preached from the pulpit that God worked like that. Some unqualified person made the contact with a potential convert and then the "more qualified" took over. We had been told not so subtly to move out of the way.

Our suspicions of how far this shoving aside would go were glaringly confirmed when the parents of one of Joe's camp friends flew from Israel for a visit and stayed in our guesthouse. Curtis had invited the parents as well as Tzafrir and his wife to join us for dinner the night they arrived. We greeted our guests, got them settled into the guest house, and waited for them to come for dinner. And we waited.

When they came for breakfast the next morning, they looked a little bewildered. They told us Tzafrir had picked them up and taken them to his house for dinner. No sooner had we started breakfast when guess who came to the door to whisk them away from us? The silent treatment and subversive tactics sent the message, "You are useless and unworthy." I felt discouraged and unwanted.

Tzafrir played this game of bait and switch a few times. I don't know if he ever realized his tactics backfired. Our visitors all thought he was weird. The biggest hurdle he faced when he tried to oust us was the fact that our kids were the ones with the connections to the camp. This meant that with every game he played, he had to use us to get his prize, the attention of the Israelis at camp.

Toward the end of the summer and the end of camp, Curtis and I were out of town when one of our kids called. Brother Tzafrir had asked about having a big fellowship for the Israelis at our house. We said that was fine. A few hours later our kids called again and said Tzafrir had asked our girls to make the food for sixty people. He gave them the Homestead credit card to pay for it. I responded, "If you're up for it."

My daughter called a little later and said that while she and one of the "more spiritual" girls were on their way to the grocery store, Tzafrir called again and told my daughter we needed to pay for the meal ourselves. She sounded exasperated on the phone, but because the fallout from Black Friday a year before had labeled us *in a bad place*, I could predict where this was all heading. For a moment or two I thought that maybe by accommodating all their demands we might be able to get back into good graces with the leadership. But my initial prediction was correct. A few hours later one of our children called to say, "Brother Tzafrir told us none of the Browns were invited to the fellowship!"

The fellowship for 60 people was going to be at our house, our kids were going to cook all the food, we had paid for it all, and now all our kids were told to stay away and have no interaction with the guests, all of whom were coming only because they were our kids' friends. If I hadn't felt so marginalized at the time, I would have laughed hard at the ridiculousness of it all.

One by one, our family was picked off and put out of commission. The leadership wanted our contacts, our money, our house, our pavilion, but they didn't want us! That was obvious. They justified their motives by saying God used us to meet people, believing those like Tzafrir had the better gifts and were appointed to lead these lost Jewish souls into the fold.

We just wanted to be their friends.

The Takeover of Max's Birthday Party

As Max's annual birthday party was approaching in 2015, Curtis received a call from Tzafrir asking if he could see the list of people invited to Max's party. The list included some of our friends who were close to Max as well as about ten of his Homestead friends. The rest of the invited included Max's camp friends. His list looked pretty much like it had for the last few years. Tzafrir rode his bike over to Curtis's office across the road from our house. That was never a good sign. That meant he wasn't happy and needed to "mention" something to Curtis. He told Curtis he had read the list of invitees and he felt Curtis was emotionally unintelligent for making such a carnal list of kids. These were Max's friends and none of the "spiritual" kids that Tzafrir had handpicked and sent to camp all summer in the guise that they were Lem's helpers. They were sent there by Tzafrir to supersede Lem and make connections with the Israelis. He cut Max's friends from the invitation list and added the ones he thought should be there. Once again, our family was shoved aside and the leadership's agenda prevailed.

Instead of the usual games, jamming, horseback riding, canoeing, and eating on the deck, Tzafrir invited the elite Homestead worship team, equipped with amplification equipment, an electric piano, and instruments of all kinds. Many ministers attended the affair along with some of Tzafrir's Jewish acquaintances and other people none of us had ever seen before. The entire evening the guests sat in carefully arranged chairs facing the Homestead singers. The musicians performed a lengthy prepared list of Israeli songs that seemed to never end. Max's camp friends had anticipated the usual fun evening on the deck and looked bored. As the worship team finally wrapped up their last song, the life drained out of me. The camp staff jumped up and told the campers to run to the cars. They had to get back to camp before their curfew. We sang a hasty "Happy Birthday" while they grabbed a piece of cake and drove off. Many of Max's camp friends said, "Sorry Max," as they ran to the car. They witnessed with their own eyes how one Homestead leader ruined a 21-year old's birthday party.

By that point, I had built up a big reserve of shame, embarrassment, fury, hopelessness, discouragement, all tumbling around in my heart and mind. Max's party brought to a head all those confusing feelings and made me want to scream, "What am I doing with my life?" I felt trapped. Without a voice.

Max's birthday was a turning point in my commitment to Homestead. I no longer trusted the flimsy, wishy-washy leadership. At times I saw them as bullies, other times as charming, and often as deceitful liars. Filled with raging bottled-up emotions, I didn't know what to do. I felt like I was going crazy. But one thing was clear to me: the bubble of deception had burst! The unraveling had begun.

Joe Becomes a Thorn in the Side

The leaders no longer wanted Curtis's input at the multitude of frequent meetings he used to be required to attend, so you might think life was less stressful, but we found ourselves inundated with what Brother Howard called a big problem: our son Joe. Joe loved riding on our 4-wheeler, but to get from one part of our property to the other to do chores, Curtis decided we needed a street legal vehicle. When Joe had a serious accident on the 4-wheeler we also needed to find a safer mode of transportation. Joe found an old Jeep to replace our totaled 4-wheeler. This Jeep had no shocks and was beat up. As was the way, Curtis asked Brother Howard permission to buy it. He said Brother Blair had one and thought it would be fine. It wasn't. One day Caleb, an up-and-coming young minister who had become close friends with Aber, Blair's son, saw Joe driving the Jeep in town and reported to a minister that Joe was "too proud" and shouldn't be allowed to drive such a vehicle. One way someone moved up the ladder at Homestead was by having *burdens* for others. He or she expressed those *burdens* to one or more ministers who then confronted the person with whatever the sin was. In this case it was Joe's pride. Pretty soon they conjectured Joe's head would be so big it wouldn't fit in the Jeep and he'd need a bus. This young minister evolved from being close to our family into a malicious person as he acquired points from the leadership at Joe's expense. We were told to get rid of the Jeep immediately. Still trying to be good Homesteaders, we did.

At any rate, we heard about the Jeep ad nauseam—long after we got rid of it. Brother Howard said it was a source of mimetic rivalry at Homestead. He never apologized for giving us permission to buy it.

Joe came under fire repeatedly because the leadership claimed he was too "business oriented" and therefore *carnally minded*. The ministers insisted on using the Jeep as an example of Joe's pride. The leaders thought he should pull nails out of old wooden beams at the Heritage Restorations lumber mill where many a young man had served his time in monotonous tedious work. Brother Howard told Curtis that Joe should quit working for Homestead Construction as a project manager building luxury homes. They felt the owners of the company weren't a qualified "covering" for Joe and building luxury homes fed his elevated ego. (At that time, Curtis was one of the two co-owners of the business.)

Because Joe was successful and smart, he became a challenge to his appointed ministers. One called him at random times to go to a *ministry* meeting where the young minister would yell at him for offenses like making too much money or leading a young person astray by answering questions about investments or the stock market. Joe became emboldened by these explosive sessions and secretly recorded some of these emotionally-charged meetings. Joe's status at Homestead sunk lower and lower. Like his brother Jonathan, he wasn't about to relinquish his dignity or discredit his character and become a slave doing someone else's bidding. He was too smart for that, but for years before he left the group, he endured the attempted mental and emotional torture at the hands of those young ministers.

The Dream that Changed Everything

Covenant was one of the main words tossed about at Homestead. We were touted as a *covenant community*, though, like many of the doctrines there, the definition seemed vague and at the same time all- inclusive. Our salvation hung on our covenant. Our motivation for success, as well as the reason for our failure, was based on how we treated "our covenant." If we displeased the leadership, we were shamed for not upholding our commitment to "the covenant."

When we joined, we didn't sign anything, and if the leaders talked to us about making "a covenant" I don't remember it. I thought we were obeying God when we joined. Brother Blair's definition of Scriptures and vocabulary words evolved over the years. He tried to bring clarity to his meaning of covenant in 2006 when he wrote a 138-page book titled, *Confession for Baptism and Communion*. He instructed us to read each commitment and sign our names to each one. We had to sign our names hundreds of times in that document before we could take communion again. I had been a member for so long that unfortunately I signed the book trusting the leadership. After all, it was required to sign it in order to remain a member. Any time a member disagreed with the leadership, committed a sin, or left Homestead, the ministers claimed they had broken their "covenant." Unfortunately, this document was the standard we were to live up to, whether it was realistically possible or not.

One night in January 2016, Curtis dreamed the exact same dream three times. He woke up startled, got out of bed pondering it, and then fell back asleep and would dream it again. That had never happened to him before and it shook him up. He had the distinct feeling in the dream that he should not sign the *Confession* any more. He didn't understand why.

After the dream, Curtis felt compelled to read the *Confession* again. The book had expanded to 168 pages by then. He found the key to his answers on page one. It said the entire *Confession* was based on the written agreement signed by all the Israelites referenced in the Book of Nehemiah, Chapter 9. When Curtis turned to Nehemiah, he saw that Chapter 10 sets out the text of the agreement Blair referred to in the *Confession*. He was struck by the verse in that chapter that the agreement was "a curse and an oath." It came to his mind that Jesus said in Matthew 5:34-37 not to make an oath at all. Oaths are "from the evil one." He realized that we had cursed ourselves by signing our names to that document.

In Nehemiah the people were proclaiming to God their allegiance to obey His commands. The Homestead *Confession*, on the other hand, included a loyalty oath to Homestead, binding not only themselves, but also their children, grandchildren, great-grandchildren, etc., to the Homestead leadership. It carried the belief that anyone born at Homestead was under God's will to be a member for life. A child would be denied their free will. When a child chose to break away from Homestead, that decision would come at the cost of splitting his family apart. Blood-born children who were not a part of Homestead were no longer family. Instead, they became children in name only because they broke away from their real family, the only thing that could save them. They had chosen to go their own way and renounced their true family. It was all or nothing at Homestead.

·

Brother Blair had us sign our names to affirm we had no question and no doubt about anything in the *literature* he had written. Yet, he himself rewrote his books over and over, and after he had rewritten them required us to return the books. Then we were required to buy the new copies. He didn't refund the purchase price of any of the books we had to dispose of. He had doubts about what he had written, but we weren't allowed the freedom to question him. By signing the oath, we agreed that if we revoked our membership and left Homestead, we were going to Hell. Our leaving meant we had turned our backs on God Himself. It was clear that Blair had set himself up as God.

Curtis was convicted by God that the *Confession* was an oath by every definition, and since the leaders believed the contrary, we had to be obedient to God and true to our conscience.

Curtis brought up his concerns about the *Confession*, but once again Brother Howard's response to Curtis's concern was, "Doctrine doesn't matter as long as you're happy and feel connected." The reliance on feelings is what got us into this mess. After Curtis confronted them, the leaders drafted a 23-page letter justifying the oath. It was nothing but a lot of words. Circular reasoning. It never addressed the Scriptures that are so simple and clear. They claimed Curtis defied God (them) by bringing up useless and frivolous opinions. Although the 168-page document we signed was all about Homestead's doctrine, when Curtis challenged Blair's use of doctrine, suddenly Curtis's failure was not focusing on his feelings. Howard once again said, "But don't you feel the presence of God in the music, the worship, and the fellowships?" If Curtis had brought up a feeling he had had, they would have responded with, "You aren't focusing on the doctrine!" This strategy of using "doctrine, and feelings" (whichever strategy worked at the time) and throwing the problem back on the one who had questioned had been used since we first visited.

Though Curtis presented the letter with sincerity and humility, the leadership labeled him as bitter, dishonorable, and a covenant breaker. He was criticized for focusing on the particulars rather than the universals. That was one of their catch-all phrases used to send you down multiple rabbit trails hoping you'd forget your original accusation.

Being an attorney and by now emboldened by the truth, he refused to drop the issues, convinced the details were of utmost importance. In his argument, Curtis raised the concern that the *Confession* made it easy for the ministers to abuse their disciples. After all, they could just condemn the disciple as rebellious, faithless, and untrusting and the ministers would never have to question their own attitudes or actions.

There was simply no way to talk about anything contrary to what Blair wanted. The leaders could not bring anything to resolution in obedience with Scripture. There were only two choices:

1. Agree with Blair's vision and words.
2. Be a "covenant breaker" and go to Hell.

I was more convinced than ever that the true church should look like a hospital where sick people came for healing. Jesus came to reconcile us to Him and each other. At Homestead issues were never resolved and relationships remained shallow and broken. Blair had instructed all ministers to never "humble themselves down." The leaders never had to care about their words because they had the *Confession* and "covenant" *as* their safety net. Because they taught that they had *the mind of Christ*, they could never be wrong. They could dish out whatever they thought and never take any responsibility. Blair expected blind submission from his followers, without regard to the truth. No one could question his authority without the fear of retaliation.

We were in Boise visiting our kids who were trying to start a new Homestead community there when Curtis told Brother Howard we were leaving Homestead. I was scared to death and walked around in a panic for days. I desperately wanted peace, but at that time, I was scared to leave. One of our kids agreed with the leaders, and said we were going to Hell if we broke our covenant. We had taught them that lie, and now we were the ones suffering for it. We'd be rejected by some of our own kids if we left and wouldn't be allowed to have a relationship with our grandkids. Brother Howard flew to Boise to talk us into staying. We tucked our tails between our legs and crawled back to Waco. We were in big trouble and Brother Howard put us on Friday night status. We could attend church on Sunday by invitation only. We'd fallen to the bottom of the ladder. Part of me felt relieved. I didn't have to start a new life just yet. I was scared of the unfamiliar joy and more comfortable with the familiar pain. We did not realize it then, but after we left the last time, we saw that the Lord used our going back in to rescue most of our kids.

Sinking Lower

I could never tell my sister Leigh all I was thinking and feeling. She hated Homestead, and for years she and her friends had prayed we'd leave. She had witnessed firsthand how my relationship with her had been torn apart over the community. She watched our family fracture when Jonathan left us. In fact, she and my brother-in-law had taken him under their wings because we had been forced to abandon him.

When Leigh's daughter Emily got engaged, Leigh planned the wedding by herself. Her husband had died of brain cancer two years earlier, so when we received the wedding invitation, I immediately responded "Yes! We wouldn't miss it!" I knew Leigh needed our help and support and I wanted to do something to ease her burden.

Three days before the wedding, Brother Howard called Curtis at midnight and definitively stated, "You are not going to that wedding!" The life drained out of me. I could literally feel my heart break. How could we do that to my sister?

We knew if we defied them again, we would be severely punished, made to *pray through* until we admitted we were wrong. We would have to grovel in repentance until they felt we had repented enough and could be allowed to attend certain meetings. They would publicly shame us and use us as an example of what happens when someone disobeys. The only way back to being in good standing would be to *prove ourselves* by publicly testifying how sorry we were, how we had let the sin of pride creep into our hearts, and then declare that we owed our lives and the chance to go to Heaven to them.

We were exhausted.

It was easier to not go to the wedding.

Leigh's sister-in-law was hosting a bridesmaid luncheon the day before the wedding. Our suddenly not going meant there would be six fewer people at the luncheon she had already planned and paid for. Unfortunately, Leigh was familiar with this scenario. We had made and canceled plans over the years to the point she never knew what to count on. Through tears, I lied to Leigh. I said we couldn't come to the wedding because Curtis' mother was sick, and she might die while we were gone. While Curtis's mother was terminally ill and died in less than a month, this was not the whole truth and Leigh knew we couldn't go because the Homestead leaders wouldn't let us go. As usual, Leigh responded graciously. And as usual, I felt remorse for what I had done.

True to form, at the next Sunday meeting Blair told the congregation that our blood relatives had the power to pull us away from *the body* more than anyone or anything because those relationships pull on our heartstrings. But, he said, our true family consisted of the members of Homestead. Those we covenanted with. He said our blood relatives are not part of the body of Christ, so why waste our time on them? They claimed the most dreaded fellowships were with family outside of Homestead. I thought, "How sad. How heart-breakingly sad." Where was the love for family?

That same day, Howard asked us, "Do you feel good about your decision to not go to the wedding?" In my heart, I shook my head no, but outwardly I nodded yes. I didn't know how to tell him the truth. Especially not to him or the other ministers. He said we were not going and that was that, but because there had been no discussion, he could confidently say that Curtis and I made the decision to not go. He wouldn't have to admit that he intimidated us and manipulated us into making the decision. It didn't matter that we had been given no alternative. One more time I had to stuff my feelings, opinions, and attitudes deep down in the box where all the discord, pain, and confusion resided underneath the remade, submissive me.

I have never regretted anything quite so much as not attending my niece's wedding. I hated myself for not being able to stand up to them, and I hated how they divided families.

A few years before her wedding, my niece thought about joining Homestead and came to visit the community for a while. Of course, this terrified my sister who wanted her daughter to have nothing to do with Homestead. Her quest ended rather abruptly when Brother Asi was preaching at the first meeting she attended and while looking straight at her, yelled, "You think you are saved, but you aren't!"

I knew the leaders believed those outside Homestead were not saved, but this was the first time I heard one of them confront an outsider about their salvation. There was nothing subtle about his words and Emily took offense. She had been raised in a Christian church and had served as a Christian missionary for a year. After the meeting I told Brother Asi that my niece was offended, and he replied that she needed to be. Emily left the next day.

A year later my daughter and her husband were passing through the town Emily lived in and went to her Sunday school class with her. The minister taught about the danger of cults, and my son-in-law felt like the lesson was pointed at Homestead. It was his turn to be offended! Brother Blair got wind of what Emily's church supposedly felt about Homestead, and he decided we needed to break off our relationship with my sister and her family.

In the days and weeks following Howard telling us we weren't going to Emily's wedding; I desperately tried to make sense of our predicament. Were we supposed to endure and overcome by succumbing to what the leaders wanted us to do and be? After all, hadn't God brought us here? Or had we been tricked into joining in the first place and now He wanted to set us free?

I was conflicted, confused and confined. I didn't dream of freedom. In fact, I had no concept of what life outside of Homestead might look like. What I did know was I couldn't live with all the turmoil much longer. The knots began to untangle when Brother Blair railed at a young minister in a church-wide meeting for something as trivial as singing what Blair considered the wrong song. I couldn't believe he was angry that he would have to be inconvenienced by someone's attempt to please him. It seemed as though Brother Blair thought the young minister should read his mind. Watching the young minister shake and drop to his knees in condemnation, I became angry that yelling at a young person in front of a thousand people seemed to be the only way the leaders knew how to correct someone at Homestead.

Sitting in the pew in the aftermath of his temper tantrum, I realized Brother Blair was sending us all a message— *Don't slip up, don't question him*. If we did, we might make him exert himself too much, and it wouldn't be good for his always failing health. It struck me that he'd been sick and about to die ever since we'd met him. On a few occasions we'd have to turn around and come home from a vacation because he was on the brink of death and, for some reason they never explained, we had to be in Waco. My grandmother was also a hypochondriac and gained a lot of attention that way. My mother, too. How many times had I been scared she was going to die?

I felt the familiar churning in my guts and wanted to run out of the building. When I looked at Brother Blair, I suddenly saw the Wizard of Oz. I could clearly see the scene where Toto pulls back the curtain, and sure enough, there was Blair pulling levers and pushing buttons while smoke spewed and thunder crashed and boomed. Just like in the movie.

That day the bubble of blindness burst. Blair could no longer bewitch me. His scare tactics snapped in half. I sighed with relief as I saw him for who he was, which was a pathetic man whom God had gifted, but, because of his own brokenness, used those gifts to meet his own needs. He had bewitched many by his spirit of control, offering the alluring appeal to *only trust me and you can live the life of your dreams – perfection on the earth.*

But he wasn't perfect, and he wasn't God. He was the wizard pressing and pulling levers and knobs of fear and intimidation. His constant promise of *something big is just about to happen; what we've been waiting for is just around the corner* kept the greyhounds chasing the ever-elusive rabbit, making his dreams come true. At the same time, our true identities were beaten to a pulp in the hopes that we would someday be a "new creation." His dreams came true by spiritually and psychologically abusing his disciples.

At that moment, "Little Dorothy" rose up inside of me, stomped her foot, and exclaimed, "Wait a minute, what you're doing is wrong! It's wrong to scare innocent people to death and call yourself God! You chase your dreams by hurting others with fear, lies, and deception."

There was no turning back. I was on my way to freedom.

Joe's Final Straw

Over the years Homestead had broken up several established religious communities by persuading a community's leadership to come under Homestead's authority. From what I could see, as a result of the Homestead leaders' involvement, these communities became fraught with condemnation and division and fell to pieces. Sometimes Homestead picked up individual members that way but usually left a long trail of confusion and broken relationships. It was like a debilitating disease infected each group Homestead tried to infiltrate. Brother Blair's biggest dream was to have a community in Israel that would be the catalyst for bringing the Jews to Jesus.

I think Blair wanted to avoid the problems he had created by trying to take over other communities, so to avert another mess, he made clear that no one was allowed to go to Israel for a vacation because our going might mess up his vision. He planned two trips to Israel for select Homesteaders. Curtis and I were on both. (Things were no different in Israel.) On our second visit to Israel, we spent time with a well-established community. The Homestead leadership flatly disagreed with much of the doctrine of this community, but they felt certain they could win over some of the young people. Some months after that trip, a group of their members came to Waco for fellowships and meetings. Then another group from Waco traveled to Israel and conducted meetings with the people in that community. Eventually, a combined group of young people started a new Homestead community in Israel. Brother Blair's dream had come true! But while Brother Blair triumphed, once again, the merging of the two communities left broken and hurting relationships behind.

Joe had made lots of friends from Israel at camp who invited him to visit. (They didn't know that Israel was "off limits" to Homestead travelers like Joe, Curtis, and me.). Unbeknownst to Curtis and me, in January 2016, Joe, who was 28 years old at the time, booked a solo trip to Israel. He had talked about wanting to go and I thought one day he probably would, but I had no idea he had the guts to go under the radar. Around that time, we had talked to Blair's son Aber about taking a family trip to Israel. He said he thought that was a great idea, but we realized permission had been denied when Brother Blair announced in a Sunday meeting that only the people he deemed qualified could go to Israel. Aber didn't have the guts to tell us to our face that we weren't allowed to go to Israel. Instead, he must have told his dad who once again used us an example to the entire congregation. He made it clear that if the wrong people went, the purposes of God could be jeopardized. And according to Blair, we were the wrong people.

Brother Blair's increased dissatisfaction with Curtis and me was undoubtedly due to Curtis telling the leaders that the Homestead "oath" was from the devil. Joe had seen how we had been treated, and probably felt empowered to defy the leadership and do something he wanted to do for a change. He took a weeklong "layover" in Israel on his way home from Boise where he had been working at his older brother's accounting firm preparing tax returns. The whole week in Israel was a harried one, but Joe didn't care. He was excited to be with his friends, though he dreaded going home to face the consequences. He knew he wanted out of Homestead but wondered what would happen to him in the outside world. All his life he had been repeatedly warned about the despicable life he would live if he broke his Homestead covenant. The ministers told the young people they would probably live a life of crime outside Homestead. This is what we all were told.

When Joe got back, the drama over his going to Israel heightened every time Curtis was called into the conference room and interrogated. The elders were convinced Curtis and I knew all along about Joe's trip and had lied to them. Because Curtis was on the outs, he was a suspect in everyone's eyes.

It never occurred to me that Joe would go to Israel on his own. I must confess, even though I worried about him being disfellowshipped, I was proud of him. I even admired him. He had the guts to defy them, and I didn't. We let these people control, manipulate, and get away with lying to us. We were bound in fear of what might happen if we didn't submit. I was so concerned with what people thought because displeasing them not only brought me their wrath, but also hours of "ministry" and shame.

Long before Joe went to Israel, Brother Tzafrir and Brother Howard told Curtis that he and I had failed as parents. Joe was the result of our "bad parenting." The ministers stripped us of our authority as Joe's *covering*, as they called it, and appointed other *coverings* over him to hold him accountable. Most of those who were to *cover* Joe weren't much older than him. True to Homestead form, they got caught up in other crises and never even talked to Joe. The ministers could never accuse Joe of committing Biblical sins because he wasn't that kind of kid, but to them, he committed the worst sin possible: he used the brain God gave him and wasn't afraid to question the Homestead leadership. His questions required too much from the leaders: the truth. And that was something they refused to give. Because they were cornered by Joe, they deemed Joe unworthy to stay at Homestead. All he wanted was to get out.

All of the leaders and one of my daughters didn't believe me when I said I knew nothing about Joe's trip. His "disobedience" quickly circulated through the Homestead grapevine. The fact that Curtis and I had left the community for a brief time became another problem. The leadership hadn't wanted anyone to know we had left Homestead because the members respected Curtis. By this time Curtis hadn't been a leader in six years, but everyone knew at one time Blair had made clear to the congregation that Curtis had proven himself trustworthy and he had helped many members with legal and accounting work without charge. If others in Homestead knew about our leaving, it could put questions in their minds about what had happened to make us leave. It was always bad for morale when members left. When it happened, the congregation endured long meetings where the leaders vilified those who left and instilled the fear that anyone who broke their covenant was on their way to Hell. They had tried to keep the fact that we had left a secret. But with Joe going to Israel in direct defiance to Brother Blair, everything came out. Which, I suppose, to the leadership meant a bigger problem than usual.

Aber had emailed Joe saying they would talk about his transgression when he returned from Israel. Instead, before Joe returned home, on the second day of his trip, Aber announced to the congregation that Joe was *disfellowshipped* for dishonoring his father. At first I didn't know what they meant and I'm sure no one in the congregation did either. Even though everyone was gossiping about Joe's trip, Aber made no mention of it. Most likely because it might make them look bad for disfellowshipping someone for going to the Holy Land! Plus, they didn't want other young people to defy travel orders and thought if they linked Joe to some other sin, eventually everyone would stop talking about his trip. Without saying it directly, they accused Joe of telling his friends that we had left Homestead. That was the truth, but the leaders were mad at him for telling the truth. They didn't want anyone to know we had left so they used Joe as their scapegoat. This public announcement was their effort to squelch everything - our leaving and Joe's trip. It was their effort to put an end to the rumors once and for all. Brother Howard stood up at the end of the meeting and loudly proclaimed, "Joe Brown is a liar!"

But Joe was the one who had told the truth. Howard was the one who lied.

To his credit, Howard said he felt terrible about accusing Joe of being a liar to the entire congregation. The day after he lied about Joe he showed up at Curtis's office. He felt horrible about what he said about Joe. He wanted to apologize. I assume the "pattern" to never "apologize down" took precedence because Howard never apologized to Joe for lying about him in front of the entire congregation. I had hope that Howard had a heart and could make things right with Joe, but he was a sycophant, and overrode his conscience and stayed loyal to Blair, his god.

Joe didn't know he had been disfellowshipped until his friend called him with a work-related question and told him. Can you imagine? My son wasn't notified that he had been *disfellowshipped* from the only group he had ever known while growing up. It would be equivalent to being kicked out of a family but never told. He found out because his friend had a work question.

After hearing the news, Joe slowly realized he was free from the harsh treatment and all the hypocrisy he had witnessed for years in the leadership. He was finally out and had no intention of being talked back into the confusion. The curses the people at Homestead prayed over him and the prophecies of doom and gloom had done their work on Joe. He had tried his best to fit in and please us, but the leadership pushed him out. As my mother would say, "They were their own worst enemy."

What Joe needed was love and support. We tried in our limited way to give that to him, but since we were still members and he wasn't, he wasn't allowed to come see us on "the Land" so we met with him under the radar. Our son took the road of trying to make sense of it by blocking out the confusion, regret, hurt, and rejection. Unfortunately, for a time our relationship with him worsened. He rightfully blamed us for getting him into Homestead in the first place. He was also mad at Curtis and me for leaving and going back, and even though it hurt, I didn't blame him.

When Joe started attending a prominent church in town, Brother Howard told Curtis it would be better for Joe to be in jail than to be going to that church. We were grateful he wanted to go to church. Many who leave, especially young people, feel so hurt and rejected that they leave church and God all together. The leadership wanted those who left to plummet into poverty and despair in hopes they would realize their only salvation was returning to Homestead. According to their teaching, returning to Homestead meant returning to God. Throughout this time, it dawned on me they didn't know how to love people. The only tactic they were good at was instilling fear in order to control. It was the fear that forced people to endure the ill treatment. We were all afraid of what would happen to us if we left Homestead. We had been utterly brainwashed in fear.

By this point my trust in the leadership at Homestead had deteriorated so much that I didn't believe a word they said. I realized the glue that held them together was to degrade anything they couldn't control. Our eyes were opened to the fact that people who had left the clutches of Homestead were slandered from the pulpit. And we knew we'd be on the list soon. If elders would rather their children be in prison than go to church, they were no role model for me. They only had evil intent in their hearts.

Now that Joe had been disfellowshipped, I knew my daughter was holding on by a thin thread. She had already told her friends she was leaving. It's truly strange looking back, but I never thought our family would experience the upheaval most others had. I assumed we'd be an exception. It's a mystery to me why I thought that.

Curtis and I didn't feel we could leave Homestead right after Joe left it. We wanted to wait for things to settle down. In the waiting, God gave me a glimmer of hope.

I Want Out

One night my closest friend at Homestead, asked me to pray with her. I never talked openly with her about my distrust of the leadership or any of the emotional and mental struggles I battled for fear of her tattling on me. Despite the veil of deception being removed from me, I still feared getting *in trouble*. Many people at Homestead prayed like God was deaf, yelling at the top of their lungs, or saying, "Thank you Jesus, or Halleluiah" repeatedly. Since Black Friday my prayers had been, "I'm sorry. Forgive me." Over and over.

That night, after telling God I was sorry for the umpteenth time, I felt His peace wash over me and I heard him ask, "What are you sorry for?" I realized I didn't know. Condemnation had set a hook inside of me and had pushed me to seek forgiveness. Slowly, as I thought about it, I realized I was sorry for *existing*. I felt Him when I sat with Him in silence. Quiet and solitude had been scarce at Homestead. Blair's vision had compelled us to thrive on activity. My mother worked incessantly to drown out the voices in her head that said she was not good enough. For thirty years I had lived in a circus of bustling activities and noise trying to prove I was good enough. The leadership literally mocked alone time or quiet time. Perhaps it was because they feared we might think for ourselves if we ever were quiet long enough. That night, I sat enveloped in His love. For the first time since we joined Homestead, I remembered in a personal way He was real. For the first time in years, I knew He *cared* about me.

That same night, I had a powerful dream. So powerful I asked a young man in the community to draw it for me. By that time I had repented for a year and a half for being a failure. I believed I was a disappointment, a total loser who had sinned beyond repair, but in my dream, God's hand held out a big stamp inscribed with the words, "Jesus Saves." I saw a pile of pieces of paper with writing on each one. They were my sins. Jesus Himself had stamped every piece of paper "Jesus Saves." All the while in the dream, I could hear the song "Jesus Saves" getting louder and louder, drowning out my fear and loneliness. I lay in my bed and wept for a long time. Those were tears of hope and thanksgiving. "Weeping may endure for a night, but joy comes in the morning." Psalm 39:5

That night I remembered that Jesus died for my sins on the cross and there was absolutely nothing I could do or say to undo what He had already done for me. All these years at Homestead I had forgotten about grace. It was never taught. In fact, the idea of grace was mocked because people who believed they were saved by grace weren't saved according to the leaders. It dawned on me that everyone inside Homestead mocked, ridiculed, and criticized everyone outside of Homestead for their beliefs. I had been brainwashed to believe no one except members of Homestead had the truth. Because of that, I had forgotten about the grace my Savior gifted me and instead carried guilt and condemnation all these years. My words and actions that the Homestead leadership considered sins were always recorded in Tzafrir's small spiral notebook which he kept in his shirt pocket, ready to remind me of what I had done wrong or to jot down any insubordination. But Jesus had stamped all my sins, "PAID IN FULL." The Casting Crowns song, "East from West" was popular at the time and I listened to it over and over, wondering if that was true for me. Could it even be possible that God really loved me? He seemed to be trying to convince me that He did.

We had believed the lie we needed those rules, *heavy* words, and tough love to weigh us down and keep us in check. It was like being paralyzed. But a small spark of hope ignited deep in my heart after that dream. After that night whenever I looked at the rendering of my dream, I thanked God that maybe I could trust Him again.

Even after the dream, I still struggled with relentless panic attacks. During one particularly bad one, I rode my bike to the sanctuary to pray. Even though we were touted as the "ideal community," there wasn't a single person in the entire fellowship that I felt the freedom to talk to. Inside the sanctuary sat an older woman and I sat beside her. She put her arms around me, kissed me on the cheek, and said, "I think you've forgotten God loves you." I will never forget the love I felt in her simple reminder. She defied the leadership's example when she told me the simple truth. The leadership freely pointed out my faults and judged what they considered my sins, but the only solution they offered was to work harder and be more loyal so I could earn my righteousness. Ephesians 2:8-9(NIV) says, *For it is by grace you have been saved, through faith, and this is not of yourselves, it is the gift of God, not by works, so that no one can boast.* She was right. God loved me, but through all the stress and confusion, coupled with my striving and trying to prove my righteousness, I had forgotten the simple truth: God loves me.

That gave me hope.

And hope does not disappoint.

Until then I had never heard anyone in all those years at Homestead say that God loved us.

Our Final Straws

Our daughter sat through the Friday night meeting trying not to cry after hearing the news from Brother Tzafrir that it was "not God's will" for her to marry the man of her dreams. She had taken the news as best as we could have hoped. Brother Tzafrir tried to assure us that the boy's dad agreed with the leadership. Like so many other similar situations, we would have to swallow the news and move on. But our daughter held out hope a little while longer. One of her friends' parents and siblings had previously left Homestead. As was common, since he was the only one left at Homestead, he was given privileges others were denied in an effort to keep him from leaving also. He was allowed to get his pilot's license and build a big house. The son Blair declared his successor, Asi, became his mentor and close friend. He knew the leadership had forbidden the marriage between my daughter and the one she loved so he decided to help my daughter get an audience with Asi. Asi agreed to meet with my daughter and listen to her story. She told him who she felt she was supposed to marry. Asi responded with, "I thought that was God's will myself. Why don't you two get married outside of Homestead, skip a few communions, and come back?"

This was unheard of advice! He was telling her to "break her covenant" by leaving Homestead, get married, and then come back. She left that meeting in high hopes. We were shocked by that advice and really wanted her to marry who she wanted. We never heard anything else from anyone in leadership about the situation. Curtis asked Howard about

Asi's advice to our daughter and he replied, "Asi never would have said that." One thing was clear: Aber, Howard and Tzafrir were determined for our daughter to never marry the man she loved.

My daughter, on the other hand, was done with the leaders' lying and manipulation. She saw right through them. They were constantly covering for themselves by using people to get what they wanted. All the while they didn't care about the people they used. She told everyone she knew she was leaving and gave them the reasons why. Of all my kids, she had a heart for those who were weak or unpopular and frequently planned fun birthday parties for those who might be overlooked. She hated to leave them behind but couldn't stand to live among hypocritical lying leaders another day. When she told an older lady that she was particularly close to that she was leaving Homestead, this *sister* took off her sweet demeanor, stood up and yelled, "Get your things and get out of my house!" and never talked to my daughter again. She justified her treatment of my daughter as obeying the leaders. In reality she had learned to be self-righteous and mean-hearted under their "ministry." This lady was in her 70's and my daughter was in her 20's. My daughter began to question if Homestead should even be called a church. No wonder so many young people who leave Homestead give up on God altogether.

One night after a typical Friday night meeting, I looked at my phone and saw a message from my daughter. It read, "Mom, I'm married." I am crying as I type this. Every time I tell the story, I cry. I was at a stupid Friday night meeting while my daughter got married! She eloped with the man she loved rather than plan a wedding knowing that the leadership would most likely not allow either of their families to attend. They sacrificed for us. Once again Homestead came between our family.

Our daughter and son-in-law decided to have a reception a year later thinking the dust would have settled by then and we all would celebrate together. Our son-in-law's parents said they would go. Our daughter and her husband sent out beautiful invitations to friends at Homestead, leaders, and family. One night Curtis and I were at our pavilion by the river at a fellowship. Aber stood near me when the subject of the wedding reception came up. He had received an invitation. I tested the waters and said, "I think everyone should go." He snarled and replied, "No one is going to that wedding reception. I mean, no one!" I'm sure he thought his stamp of disapproval put an end to the dilemma as the leadership saw it. If they allowed members to attend, they might set a precedent. They might even lose control.

We had told our daughter we would go to her reception as she and her husband planned it a year after the wedding hoping to bring peace and unity to their families and Homestead. After all, Asi had suggested they leave Homestead and get married and hopefully come back. Although Howard, Tzafrir, and Aber never believed he said that. Both families had agreed to attend the reception the year before, but by the time the reception rolled around everyone was afraid to talk about it, much less go. One by one our Homestead kids backed out. Even our son-in-law's parents backed out. Fear of the reprisal for disobeying the leadership loomed over everyone who received an invitation.

Curtis talked to Asi about us going to the reception. We knew about his advice to our daughter, but we also knew the rest of the leaders would say a flat NO about attending the reception. After Blair appointed Asi as his successor, Asi seemed to be grooming the congregation by appearing to be more accommodating and open-minded. He told Curtis, "If you feel like it's God's will, you should go. No one should tell you what to do." Hmm. That wasn't the way it had ever worked in thirty years, but we took him at his word. In fear and trepidation, we got in the car with one of our sons and headed to Dallas for the reception.

We had been in the car for maybe twenty minutes when Brother Howard called. Curtis told him we were on our way to the reception.

Long silence. Then a deep groan. "I can't believe you would do that!" he exclaimed in his overly dramatic way, making sure we felt his displeasure. Of course, he couldn't believe we would defy them. We never had. This was our first time to cross their will. I was scared to death. And a tiny bit elated. We had crossed a line into the end zone, like we had made a touchdown. But the game wasn't over yet.

The next day was one of two communion services we had each year. This was the service that drew the line between the committed and those on the fence. Matt, our son-in-law, a young minister and best friends with Asi, called first thing on Sunday morning and said he "couldn't take communion with us" because we had gone to our daughter's reception. That meant he felt we should be disassociated or disfellowshipped. Soon after, Howard called to say Lisa, our daughter's mother-in-law, said she couldn't take communion with us either because we had rebelled and gone to the reception. I can say the reception was beautiful, but I was a nervous wreck the entire night knowing all Hell would break loose as soon as everyone found out we had gone. The leaders must have been up half the night discussing what they should do with us. We had already caused them grief but Curtis was someone they needed to use discretion with because he knew too many people outside of Homestead and could potentially harm their reputation they so closely guarded. They knew Curtis had nothing to hide. They couldn't blackmail him.

Somehow they allowed us to take communion, probably because it was easier than having to explain to the congregation why we weren't there. By then Curtis and I understood firsthand that the leaders routinely weaponized church meetings and the Lord's Supper. This practice had manipulated and harmed many fragile people before us. They willingly distorted who God is to force obedience to them. And like similar groups, they did it in God's name.

Hell's Kitchen

We had heard the story of the beginnings of Homestead from the time we visited until we left. Blair included the story of their humble and curious beginnings into scores of books he wrote, each video he produced, talks at music programs, fairs, and many sermons he preached. He told of how he had cleaned urine off the walls of their first meeting place, the original Labor Temple in Hell's Kitchen on East 14th street in Manhattan. They met in a converted discotheque that formerly had a three-story picture of Satan painted on the walls. This narrative conveyed to the members that his sacrifice paved the way for us to come along and be a part of the great continuum. Our leader suffered so that we didn't have to. Sound familiar? His story included how they left everything familiar and lived in an unsafe apartment building with long ochre hallways where lonely people were stabbed in fights or raped and caught on fire with lighter fluid. He and Regina sacrificed by living in a cold water flat.

For the first twenty years we were at Homestead we never dreamed Blair would lie to us. When my cousin, who is married to a longtime native Manhattan resident, came to visit in 1998, we took them to the 25th anniversary celebration where we watched a video Blair had made. After it was over my cousin said, "East 14th street is not in Hell's Kitchen." I trusted Blair so much that I argued with her until she gave up. I mentioned it to Howard, and he just glossed over the topic. We learned that Hell's Kitchen is one of the most well-known neighborhoods with well-defined boundaries on the map of New York City since 1859.

About the time we were making our escape from Homestead, one of the young people who had left Homestead years before went sightseeing in New York City. Having grown up hearing about the heroic efforts Blair and Regina had gone to in establishing the community, this young man went to see the place where Homestead had its meager roots. He was shocked to find out the building formerly called the Labor

Temple where Blair's church met was actually a 45-minute drive from Hell's Kitchen. Cold water flats were outlawed in the 50's. This young man's revelation about Hell's Kitchen revealed that Blair had been lying to us for years. My cousin had been right and we had looked like fools to blindly follow someone who preyed on others' trust. Curtis added Hell's Kitchen to the bottom of his long list of questions. Blair's sons, Aber and Asi, had various responses. They admitted the question about Hell's Kitchen had come up years before. They didn't say what the conclusion was. They said it was "like Hell's Kitchen." That meant it was a rough part of the city, rather than the name of the neighborhood, but they didn't admit that it was a lie. They finally accused Curtis of being too picky. Was he really willing to go to Hell over capital letters, they asked? They never admitted that their father had lied to thousands of people. They couldn't because he wasn't *like* God. He was their God.

Jesus Coming in the Flesh

Recently during a sermon, a pastor held up a mug that said, "I can do all things in Christ by taking a Scripture out of context." That pastor said a lot of harm has been done by doing just that. We knew that to be all too true at Homestead. Years ago Blair threw out the phrase, "Jesus coming in the flesh," and would imply that people could be Jesus coming in the flesh, like when a Christian helps someone, he could be said to be the hands and feet of Jesus. Many years ago he wrote a piece of literature that basically said the elders of Homestead were Jesus coming in the flesh. His revelation must have been met with some resistance and he decided the congregation wasn't ready for that truth just yet, so he had everyone turn that piece of literature back in. From time to time he would say we just weren't ready for his new revelation and chastised us by teaching that we were like babies and still needed milk and hoped that one day we would be mature and want meat. Things would rock along for a while with no mention of Jesus coming in the flesh and then he would test the waters again. He told the congregation that his writings rewired our brains because it was like a different language, for the spiritually mature. In reality he always left the reader wondering what on earth he was trying to say. I came to the conclusion that everything he wrote could be summed up, "You will find the Kingdom of God by trusting and submitting to me. Homestead is the answer to all the world's problems."

Another bubble burst when Blair published, *Is the Church Christ on Earth*? in response to the question from outsiders if he believed Homesteaders were the only saved people on earth. Blair claimed Homestead was the only *fitly framed* church on earth. That was Blair's way of answering, "Yes, Homestead congregants were the only saved people on earth."

The theme of this new book claimed that the church is Christ on the earth. All of his previous literature was so convoluted you could interpret it in a myriad of ways, but this book made clear that he and his hand-picked leaders are Jesus in the flesh. After we were required to read the book, Brother Tzafrir would frequently say, "And we have the mind of Christ," as he motioned with his arms, indicating he and the leaders were the only people who had the mind of Christ. Another one of the leaders claimed that since the leaders had the mind of Christ, they could not be wrong. Having wrestled with the leadership for the last several years over broken contracts, legal infractions and lies, Curtis was done trying. Blair had used the same tactic that others before him had used to snare the vulnerable and broken, "The church in America has failed, so join me in resurrecting the real body of Christ." Also like those cult leaders before him, Blair had twisted Scripture, made up his own doctrine, lied and manipulated people to get what he wanted.

The reality that Blair really thought he was Jesus in the flesh should have been enough for us to break ties with Homestead. But when the leaders began to act like they were God and hurt our two youngest children, we saw how this distorted belief played out in real time. Our two youngest were driving to town one night after attending a youth meeting. Our daughter had her Bible on her lap, and they were singing a Christian song when a police car pulled them over because one of the car's tail lights was burned out. The officer didn't give our son a ticket; he just said to replace the light. Asi happened to be driving behind our kids and saw the police pull our son over. At the time Homestead was going through one of its many crises because someone was recording church meetings and they were being leaked to the public. As usual, this meant Homestead was being "persecuted" and "attacked by the devil." This time it was by a traitor inside Homestead since Sunday meetings were closed meetings where no one other than members were allowed to attend. When Asi witnessed the police stopping our kids, he immediately had a "revelation from God" that our son was the perpetrator. The next day our son was accused of secretly recording the meetings. At Homestead you were always guilty until proven innocent. This particular kid of ours would be the last one to do something subversive like that. The leaders wouldn't let up and continued to force him to admit that he had done it. He felt shamed by the blame they continued to heap on him and to this day carries the wounds the leaders inflicted on him. (All because Asi had convinced himself that God spoke to him that our son was guilty.) He believed he was Jesus and had the right to accuse an innocent person because he could not be wrong.

Blair had a severe problem with anger and demonstrated it publicly for years, always making the excuse that he was expressing "God's" wrath. Many like our son had suffered from condemnation and rejection and many had lost their faith completely because one broken, confused man claimed to be Jesus. So many had lied for him and covered up gross sin so as not to upset him by tainting the reputation of the kingdom he had built.

For a long time we had believed we had joined a church that functioned like the body of Christ should. We had foolishly sacrificed our own hopes and dreams for Blair. We naively gave up our rights for one person who was nothing like the Jesus who suffered and died on the cross. The leaders and all members did all in their power to keep Blair from suffering. That was the ultimate goal at Homestead. To keep Blair happy.

While Jesus came to ease our suffering, Blair caused the suffering of many of his followers.

I remember Regina telling me the answer to all our problems was to submit and serve Blair's vision. Our service to the greater whole would swallow up our personal issues. Focusing on the big picture was the same strategy every dictator and cult leader have used. It worked at Homestead as long as our service pleased Blair because our lives only had meaning in the context of sacrificing for his vision. Focusing on personal needs was condemned as selfish and faithless.

Attempting to question or understand Blair's vision was characterized as impeding God's will on the earth. This strategy kept Blair and his appointed disciples above reason and relationship. They couldn't be wrong so the response to sin on their part was to absolve it by quoting a Scripture like, *Love covers a multitude of sins. 1 Peter 4:8(NIV)*

There was never any reconciliation between leaders and members. We just accepted the injustice as part of our cross to bear and moved on by letting the big picture swallow up our lives. We started out looking for a church and thought we had found Nirvana. On Black Friday, God took me by the shoulders and shook me until my teeth rattled. Curtis and I had been diehard members for years. We worked hard to keep up the right image. We gave it our all. The bubble burst when we faced the truth. By 2016 our trust had eroded to the point that we felt we had no true rapport with anyone in leadership. Blair's outbursts of anger and his mistrust of those who disagreed with him added to our awakening. He finally admitted what he thought all along that he was *Jesus in the flesh*. That was the final straw. The hard truth.

Our Last Supper

For our last two years at Homestead, I jumped when the phone rang. Every time I thought about our exodus my heart hammered, and I held my breath. I couldn't shake the dread of the unknown. Or face my two daughters I'd be leaving behind. Everything in me wanted to scoop them up and take them with me. I could hardly bear leaving my precious grandkids behind, knowing I wouldn't be allowed to see them. I didn't mind so much that we'd be called Judases, betrayers, and covenant breakers. Knowing all the lies they'd fill my kids and grandkids with was what got to me. I'd never be able to tell them my side of the story. I hated that division. Them versus us. In spite of the consequences, we knew it was time to escape. I'd had a descriptive and disturbing dream years before we left. In the dream, these two daughters were in a car leaving a large complex like a hotel with a conference center. The older one drove away as I ran alongside the car imploring them, "Keep praying, don't stop, keep trusting God, don't give up!" Over and over, I exhorted them until the car sped up and merged onto the highway. I walked back toward the hotel watching the ocean on my right. A huge wave rose over me, and I prayed the girls had driven far enough away that it would not overtake them. I woke up praying for my daughters. I couldn't shake the feeling that we were being separated by something big and ominous. Leaving Homestead 15 years later was the *something big*. Our punishment for leaving was cutting us off from them and our grandchildren.

But we had to leave. We couldn't pretend anymore. The leaders knew we'd passed the point of no return. Besides our two daughters, all the rest of our remaining family were determined to leave with us. They had the most to lose. The boys would lose their businesses because every person who had signed a contract with our Realtor son would break their contract and every client our CPA son had would drop him. They'd have to start all over. They'd have no friends because they'd grown up at Homestead and had few friends outside of it. My heart hurt for them because they were scared of the unknown life outside of Homestead. They'd grown up being told there were no Christian people outside of Homestead and that everyone was out to hurt them. The brainwashing covered their entire lives. At least we knew the real God and had friends before we joined. Even still, I knew we'd all be disoriented.

I couldn't imagine how I could pack up my house without help. We planned to send our youngest to live with her sister in Dallas. Her brother would live with an elderly couple in town, so that would leave Curtis and me alone for the first time in a long time. We lived on Homestead land and didn't know if they'd kick us off the land we had bought for them like they had others. Curtis and our two sons planned to tell our son-in-law after we had dinner on Sunday night. For the first time Curtis would have the freedom to tell him all the reasons he felt compelled to leave. We all hoped our son-in-law would leave with us.

That weekend, we were invited for dessert for Brother Howard's birthday a few hours before it started. We most certainly were an afterthought. When we arrived, everyone was getting up from the dinner table. We were the only ones who were invited for only dessert. I felt awkward and out of place among these people I'd known for three decades. Perhaps inviting us was their last-ditch effort to help us come back into the fold. Maybe they didn't realize how far we had fallen down what they would call the "slippery slope" to Hell.

I dreaded going because I knew we were leaving the next day, but I'm glad I went. Since the spell that held me captive had broken, I had new eyes. I no longer accepted and assumed. Now I questioned and discerned.

It seemed our presence put a damper on the evening and I saw the scene as surreal. All of the attention they had at one time lavished on our needy hearts was now turned away from us. They had used us up: our money, our time and our emotions. And because of fear we had allowed them to. Like a giant vacuum packer, they had sucked our lives dry. One elder whispered to another one in front of us which seemed so rude. Before, I would have felt part of something. It would have been great if it was Curtis who was being whispered to. His inclusion meant he knew some top-secret information about a situation that was going on. But that night, I sat there and thought to myself, "These just are not my people." They had nothing to talk about besides all the visitors from Baylor they had wowed with their wisdom. Everything centered on themselves and their financial or evangelical success as a community.

The conversation toward the end of the evening concerned a 50-year commemorative celebration being held at Baylor honoring Billy Graham. Howard derided the gathering celebrating Billy Graham's ministry and mockingly dubbed it a waste of time. Another leader seemed baffled and asked, "What on earth do they do at something like that?" Howard responded, "Nothing. Absolutely nothing at all." End of discussion.

I looked at that group and felt sorry for them. They genuinely believed they were better than Billy Graham. My grandmother would have rolled over in her grave. She adored Billy Graham. Even my mother, who hated the Baptist church, loved it when Billy Graham cut the ropes that separated the black people from the white. But Homestead's leaders never acknowledged good in any other church or ministry. That would go against their doctrine of preeminence.

Two years before the last supper at Homestead, during the time of terrible turmoil amidst panic attacks and bouts of depression, I had a dream that I held onto with the little strength I had. In the dream Curtis and I were in a small airplane flying over a beautiful canyon. A river ran through the canyon and from my vantage point it looked small, like a dark narrow ribbon winding through the canyon. Suddenly, Curtis jumped out of the plane! I knew I had to jump, but I made every excuse imaginable. “It’s too far. I’ll die or break every bone in my body. I might hit a boulder and crack my head open.” And yet, finally, I jumped. I yelled out my fears: “I’ll sink to the bottom and drown. The sheer force from jumping from such a height will kill me.” I hit the water, sank and looked up. I could see an intensely beautiful blue sky. Colorful bubbles danced around me as the sunlight hit them as I came to the surface. I popped out of the water and locked eyes on Curtis. We smiled and then laughed out loud. We felt unspeakable joy!

That dream was a gift to me. Deep inside my shattered heart I knew there was joy in the future. In my mind’s eye I could see Jesus waiting expectantly to give me a wonderful gift. I clung to that dream.

Part Four

Life after Bondage

Keep a sharp eye out for those who take bits and pieces
of the teaching you have learned and use them to make trouble.
Give these people a wide berth. They have no intention of living
for our Master Christ. They are only in this for what they can get
out of it and aren't above using pious sweet talk to dupe unsuspecting innocents.

Romans 16:17-18 (The Message)

Our daughter was devastated when her husband informed her that Curtis and I had severed ties with Homestead. We knew she'd undergo pressure from the leaders to break all ties with us. From the pulpit the ministers would claim they had done their part to "help" us. They would claim Curtis's long list of questions were frivolous and just excuses for a way to escape the discipline he needed. I heard in the next edition of the *Confession for Baptism and Communion* they labeled us wolves. Once again, I found myself *beyond emotion*. Part of me ached for my daughters and grandchildren still in, not wanting to leave them where they wouldn't thrive. And the other part of me felt paralyzed at the thought of freedom from something that had controlled our lives for so long.

The day we left I gathered some courage and called a friend in Waco. I desperately needed a friend and Jane's name came to me. I timidly told her we had left Homestead, then held my breath as I waited for her response. Immediately she invited me to have lunch that day. I still couldn't say the word "cult" or speak negatively about my experience at Homestead. I still felt invisibly bound by my commitment to uphold the honor of the order, but I felt her unspoken understanding and compassion. Jane became a real friend that day. She was the first gift I received after we left. Later, she organized a Mary Kay party for me with a group of her friends so I could learn how to apply makeup again! She even blessed me with a birthday lunch with some of her sweet friends because she knew I didn't have any of my own.

Homestead had drilled into us that there were no good people beyond their membership. I knew all along that wasn't true because I knew the people in my life before we joined were still the same wonderful people after we left, but our children and the young people who grew up there didn't have that advantage. They needed real friends like Jane was to me.

Even though we wanted to leave Homestead for a few years, our hasty departure still came as a shock to my system. I was scared for the future. I felt upended by that unfamiliar feeling of freedom. Leaving a cult is not easy. Integrating back into society was like slowly getting into a cold swimming pool. You put your hand in the water to see just how cold it really is. Then you might stand on the shallow step and get used to that, and then step down to the next step and down to the next step until you are standing on your tippy toes in the shallow end. My brain has slowly been rewiring. At first every time my phone rang my heart raced and the hair on my arms raised up as I tried to remember what I had said to so and so. I had lived that way for such a long time that I still believed I was in trouble. Even recently I got an email about a zoom meeting, and for a day I worried that someone needed to confront me! Spying a Homesteader in a store sent me into fight or flight mode. And yet, the more I recognized the lies I had believed and exchanged them for the truth, gradually the joy I had in the dream about jumping out of the airplane started taking up residence in my heart. The Bible says *the joy of the Lord is your strength*, and the more joy I felt, the stronger I became.

At first when people asked me, "What brought you to Waco?" I'd pause and reluctantly say, "Homestead." Their eyes would grow wide, and they'd ask me, "What was it like?" I'd hem and haw and try to sidestep the truth. One day I flat out said, "It's a cult." It was such a relief to have the truth come out. Instead of feeling anxious or weary, admitting Homestead was a cult made me feel like I was finally back to reality. And it started me on a journey of freedom.

Recently we attended a family wedding at a Homestead satellite community. I braced myself at the thought of seeing so many of the people I wrote about in this book, but I shouldn't have worried. When I saw them, I felt nothing but love for them. I was reminded that there are women who are still members and others who have left the group that I mistreated when I was in leadership there. On many occasions the leaders sent me to *minister* to people I barely knew. I obediently did their dirty work and hurt people in the process. At the time I didn't realize how I made others feel because I was so focused on trying to survive in the system myself! We all were. Life at Homestead was the classic "kicking the dog" scenario.

My prayer for as long as I can remember has been for God to make me the person He called me to be. At Homestead I turned into someone I was not supposed to be. God made us in His image and endowed us with unique gifts that fulfill our purpose on earth when we use them. The freedom to use those gifts to the full was denied at Homestead. I allowed myself to be stuffed into a one size fits all mold. Living in fear stifled creativity, so our gifts weren't allowed to flourish. We weren't really living; we were only surviving. The truth is this: *We are God's masterpiece. He has created us anew in Christ Jesus, so we can do the good things He planned for us long ago. Ephesians 2:10 (NLT)*

A member at Homestead told me recently they had thought about leaving the group, but when they looked at the mess some had become after leaving, they decided to stay. They didn't want their lives to fall apart like others had. This person has swallowed the Homestead lie that their only hope of living a clean and successful life is being a member there. Homestead teaches this as "relying on God," but in reality, it is "relying on patterns and false doctrine" to keep everyone in check. People decide not to leave because they are scared to risk trusting completely in God for fear that He might not be enough. It says in 2 Peter 1:3-9, (NLT) *By his divine power, God has given us everything we need for living a godly life. We have received all of this by coming to know him, the one who called us to himself by means of his marvelous glory and excellence. And because of his glory and excellence, he has given us great and precious promises. These are the promises that enable you to share his divine nature and escape the world's corruption caused by human desires. In view of all this, make every effort to respond to God's promises. Supplement your faith with a generous provision of moral excellence, and moral excellence with knowledge, and knowledge with self-control, and self-control with patient endurance, and patient endurance with godliness, and godliness with brotherly affection, and brotherly affection with love for everyone. The more you grow like this, the more productive and useful you will be in your knowledge of our Lord Jesus Christ. But those who fail to develop in this way are shortsighted or blind, forgetting that they have been cleansed from their old sins.*

The leadership didn't trust me to make wise decisions because, as they continuously reminded me, my heart was deceitfully wicked. While an unredeemed heart may remain wicked, Homestead leaders failed to believe the miracle that happens at salvation! 2 Corinthians 5:17, *(ESV) Therefore, if anyone is in Christ, he is a new creation; the old has passed away, behold, the new has come.* It says in Ezekiel 36:26-27, (NIV) *I will give you a new heart and put a new spirit in you; I will remove from you your heart of stone and give you a heart of flesh.* The Holy Spirit lives inside of us when we welcome Jesus into our lives and He transforms us by the renewing of our minds. Romans 12:2 says that we're still sinners, but our regenerated hearts have the capacity to be pliable in the hands of our savior. Only Jesus' sacrifice on the cross saved me. My salvation was not dependent on my loyalty and obedience to anyone else. Christ alone.

Homestead taught that it was the Kingdom of God. But the Kingdom of God is not a particular place or people. Like Jesus said in Luke 17:21, (NLT) *The Kingdom of God can't be detected by visible signs. You won't be able to say, 'Here it is,' or 'it's over there!' For the Kingdom of God is among you.* (Jesus living inside us) I lived in fear, condemnation and striving, but *the Kingdom of God is not a matter of eating and drinking (patterns) but righteousness, peace and joy in the Holy Spirit. Romans 14:17 (NLT) There is therefore now no condemnation for those who belong to Christ Jesus. And because you belong to Him, the power of the life-giving Spirit has freed you from the power of sin that leads to death. Romans 8:1-2 (NLT)*

For a while I thought, "Well, my experience at Homestead wasn't as bad as some peoples' traumatic experiences," and I'd try to just keep going. I realized that even though I had learned a lot of lessons while I was there, my responses to situations surprised me, almost to the point of alarming me. I would overreact when I encountered certain people and situations or had seemingly innocuous conversations with someone. Since leaving, with help from some amazing friends, I realized my confusing emotions were coming from unhealed wounds and years of living in an environment of fear and condemnation. I had no idea who I really was or how to change. God in His goodness surrounded me with His people who loved me, listened to me, and never judged me. These friends created a safe, secure place for me to process. They prayed blessings over me and taught me to bless others I might have been bitter toward. They poured unconditional love into me and taught me to listen to God's voice and know firsthand that He loves me. My brain began to be rewired and transformed. I can tell I'm growing up because I don't have as radical or frequent reactions to situations as I did. My brain is more synchronized, and my emotions are more regulated. Believe me, I've got a long way to go, and I still mess up, but to the extent I choose to live in the Kingdom of God, knowing He has provided everything I need for eternity, I feel peace and contentment. In my freedom, I've learned I can be brutally honest with God and can carry on a conversation with Him. He delights in having conversations with His children. When I feel untethered to Him, I remember the picture He gave me one day when I asked Him to show me what He thought of me. I saw myself cowering at the foot of His huge throne. He said, "What are you doing down there? Come up here!" I climbed up and He took me in His arms and held me. He offers that love to all of us.

I thought I was free when I joined Homestead, but when the spell was broken, I realized at Homestead I was only free from having to think critically, from making my own decisions, free from responsibility and free to let others do my thinking for me. I was also free to be a hypocrite and think I knew better than anyone else. If I conformed and never questioned, I'd be free to live a cozy life. But then I'd be free from an intimate relationship with my Savior. There would always be a man between God and me. I'd be free from living in freedom. Galatians 5 (NLT) says it best: *So Christ has truly set us free. Now make sure that you stay free and don't get tied up again in slavery to the law. If you are trying to make yourselves right with God by keeping the law, you have been cut off from Christ! You have fallen away from God's grace...... What is important is faith expressing itself in love. You were running the race so well. Who has held you back from following the truth? It certainly isn't God, for he is the one who called you to freedom. This false teaching is like a little yeast that spreads through the whole batch of dough. I am trusting the Lord to keep you from believing false teachings. God will judge the person, whoever he is, who has been confusing you… For you have been called to live in freedom.*

Being a follower of Jesus can be messy. Sometimes we get off course like I did for thirty years! But God is faithful to say, "What are you doing down there? Come on up here and let me hold you. I'll give you my people to teach you to walk again. I'll bind up your wounds and help you rewire your brain. That's why I sent my son Jesus to die for you. I've loved you all along. Don't ever forget that."

A Picture of Transformation and Hope

My son Jonathan, my eight-year-old granddaughter Reagan, and I scoured the beach for sharks' teeth while the sun was setting over the Atlantic. Jonathan had picked me up at the airport. He greeted me with outstretched arms and a big smile. I melted into his big burly chest so thankful for this amazing human being. I didn't deserve his enthusiastic welcome. I didn't deserve to hear his laugh and spend time with him and his three precious children. Later that evening as we walked on the beach, I watched Jonathan sift through little piles of shells looking for sharks' teeth while Reagan chased translucent crabs that scurried along the sand, yelling for me to come and see. I stood there in the dim light barely able to see anything at all through the salt spray forming on my glasses. My heart could see though. Listening to Reagan squealing with delight, I saw redemption. I saw a love that never gave up even when we tried to extinguish it. We raised Jonathan at Homestead where he never fit in. His gifts and talents didn't match the "vision" the leader had for him. We forced him to choose between us and "the world." It's a miracle he still loves us.

I found myself drawn to small pieces of sea glass and smooth stones on the beach and saw my journey in them. The wine or beer bottles and rocks had been broken and smashed and tumbled around for a long time, their original form no longer recognizable. They'd been worn smooth, the sharp edges ground off by the gritty sand on the ocean floor. The turbulent waves had tossed them on shore like Jonah being spewed out of the big fish. I saw how God had taken me through storms and turbulent times and brought me safely to shore. I don't look quite like I did when I started out. He's had to sand off many rough places in my character, and some parts that I had willfully erected, He had to mercifully shatter. I was struck by the diversity of colors and shapes and sizes of the shells and stones around my feet and thought of God's people everywhere belonging to one big amazing family. Buried inside of all of us are unique gifts and purposes that God planned before the foundation of the world. He redeemed us to restore us so we can be the people He called us to be in the first place. That's what Jesus did on the cross for you and me.

Acknowledgements

For years I ignored the dozens of people who told me I ought to write a book until one night at an event in Dallas. I was sitting at a table with some of my kids and other people I didn't know. My daughter and I had gone out in the hall of the hotel to see someone and when I came back Pastor Joe, who I did not know, sitting a few seats away got up, leaned over to me, and said, "I haven't been able to concentrate on what the speaker is saying. You have a book inside of you and you need to write it!"

I sat stunned and said to the Lord, "Ok, Ok, I'll do it."

How many times have I wished God would write me a message in the sky? Well, He did. Then and there I had to choose to obey His voice. I didn't want to want to write a book. Some of my kids just wanted to start their lives over and pretend Homestead never happened. I had spent thirty years pretending and there was so much inside I needed to sort out. Writing this book has been part of the sorting. I had to face every ugly thing about who I had become, what a terrible mother I had been, and how I needed to forgive and be forgiven. The hardest person to forgive was myself.

I must have said a thousand times when asked when my book would be finished, "I'm almost done." Thank you to all of you who have cared that I was writing this book. You have been patient and have spurred me on. It's hard to believe it's finally done.

There are so many I want to thank and some of you go unnamed. You are the ones who have prayed for me to write this book in hopes that your children and friends might be free from the Homestead spell. Thank you for encouraging me.

I am so thankful for the night at a restaurant in Cuba when I explained to the person sitting next to me that I needed someone who would hold my hand, put me on a schedule and hold me accountable and help me put together the book I was working on. Kat Caldwell looked at me and said, "Well that's what I do for a living." Doesn't God meet our needs in the most unlikely ways? I would never have finished this book without you. I know I've said it before, but I'll say it again, "I am so thankful for you!" You are the answer to my prayer. Not only are you my coach, you are my dear friend.

To my spiritual direction group: God knew when we met over fifty years ago how much I'd need you the last seven years. The early morning drives to Dallas were always worth it. I will always treasure our time together.

To Marsha Kendall, an amazing woman of God who spoke life into me on my neighbor's back porch, and when you didn't even know I was thinking of writing a book you said, "And when you write your book...." This world needs more women like you!

Thank you to those of you involved with Novo for teaching me I have authority in Christ. The Spiritual Authority Cohort brought those long-forgotten truths and practices back into my life.

Cindy Janecka, you are dear to me. The encouragement and help you've given has been invaluable. The trips to the beach gave me the space at my favorite place to pray and think and write. The way you put no limits on God has inspired me to pray big bold prayers. Remember the day I reluctantly gave all the shells I had collected to the lady who hadn't found any? The Lord spoke to me and said, "If you give them away, I'll give you better ones." And the next day He did just that! Those shells sit on my coffee table as a reminder of you and the abundant provision of God!

Thank you to my Arise Bible study group. I'm so thankful God let me be a part. Kristin Hill, you are an amazing leader and friend. I thank you for cheering me on over the finish line. And all you Julies, Kim, Lisa, Gail, Elizabeth, and all the rest are special gifts to me. Each of you love so well and have encouraged me to be bolder in my faith.

To my pickleball friends, I confess on many occasions I have chosen to be with you rather than sitting in front of the computer. You all are so much fun and have been a huge encouragement.

To Cathy Pleitz, my friend with a heart of understanding. Thank you for spurring me on and connecting me to some of the wonderful people I mention in these acknowledgements. You are tenacious and oh, so kind.

To Jan Boucek, my lifelong friend, thank you for spurring me on. You are a treasure to me. We pick up where we left off no matter how long it's been. And we think so much alike! I love you.

To Joycelyn Romero, you are my example of a servant. God has knit us together through horses and shared experiences. Your insight and depth have been an inspiration.

To my friend Jane, thank you for picking me up and helping me get reoriented. You will forever be a big part of my story.

To Patti Evans, my dear friend and roommate. Thank you for taking so much of your precious time to proofread in the most random places and at odd times on our trip to Bangladesh. I'll always see us standing in the galley on that forever long flight from Dubai using a phone for a flashlight going over the final edits.

To Sheila Everett, my mentor and friend. Thank you for your example of what a Christian is!

To Susan Jarrett and Margaret Scott, I am so thankful we are friends again. God is so good!

Sweet Emily, thank you for letting me share your story. I'm sorry you had to live it, but so glad you fled when you did.

To all my ex-Homestead friends, thank you for the myriad ways you have helped with this book. Your suggestions, using your gifts and talents have blessed me beyond what I can express. I'm so thankful for friends like you. We're like a club. We really get each other.

To all of you who proofread and gave me invaluable suggestions. Thank you for investing yourselves in this book. Each of your unique perspectives helped make my story more relatable. I thank God for all of you.

To those who have parents or children at Homestead and have reached out to me, thank you for patiently waiting for this book. I pray it helps give you a framework for those you love who are stuck in the Homestead web. Keep up the prayers!

To all my wonderful kids, I love each of you more than you can imagine. I hurt when you hurt, and I keep praying you will be restored and fulfilled by being the very unique people God created you to be. You are gifts to this world.

To my grandkids, you have brought great joy to Bapa and me. As you grow up, hang on to Jesus and the freedom He died for.

Lastly, to Curtis, thank you for graciously sending me off to the beach to write and patiently loving me when I have not been lovable. I know I went down hard with every suggestion. You were right most of the time. Thank you for being a steady, faithful rock in my life. We have weathered some storms together and been blessed beyond comprehension. I love you.

Some Final Thoughts

The way a separatist group like Homestead operates is by claiming to have all the truth. This so-called "truth" is touted as new revelation. It's a mixture of twisted Scripture and the leader's made-up doctrine. The leader claims he is directly accountable to God and no one else. He refuses to receive advice or criticism. Any attempt to correct the leader is thought of as "persecution." The leader's made up "patterns," or rules keep everyone in check. These "patterns" have to do with external aspects of life, like hairstyles, clothing or boy/girl relationships. The leaders consistently and publicly judge and criticize everyone and everything outside of the group. This includes every church denomination and faith background. A personal relationship with God is mocked as "having your own thing going with God." Each member's salvation depends on his submission to a minister "over them." If anyone breaks their allegiance to Homestead, they are condemned to Hell from the pulpit. This habitual judgment and criticism creates a culture of negativity and fear. These public examples keep the members loyal to the leaders to avoid being the subject of their criticism. Loyalty to the leaders is paramount. In order to stay in good standing, the members will cover and lie for their leaders. This leads to a culture of cover-up. All manner of sin is covered up. Everyone, especially the leaders, will lie to keep up their reputation in the public. Their financial survival depends on it. This atmosphere causes the vulnerable who genuinely want to know God more intimately, to doubt themselves, their own salvation experience, and submit to the leaders' whims. The members sincerely believe their submission to these leaders is their salvation. They give up their true identities in Christ and become identified as "Homesteaders," not Christ-followers.

If you realize you've been a victim of spiritual abuse, I've included some resources that have helped me on my own healing journey.

Activating Prayer Cohort/Novo.org

Living Fearless by Jamie Winship; Identity Exchange

Anatomy of the Soul by Curt Thompson

Understanding Spiritual Abuse by Karen Roudkovski

Redeeming Power: Understanding Authority and Abuse in the Church by Diane Langberg

For more please visit counterfeit-culture.com

Made in the USA
Coppell, TX
04 November 2025

62477032R00109